# ANTIQUE SECRETS

## Joe Willard

© 1998

Published by

 krause
publications

700 E. State Street • Iola, WI 54990-0001

Please call or write for our free catalog. Our toll-free number to place
an order or obtain a free catalog is 800-258-0929 or please use our
regular business telephone 715-445-2214 for editorial comment and
further information.

Library of Congress Catalog Number: 98-87279
ISBN: 0-87341-722-4
Printed in the United States of America

# Contents

# Acknowledgements

Thanks for all your help!

First of all to my wife whose expertise and patience were necessary as my assistant to this project. She has been the best partner I could have ever hoped for as we went out to do all of these things.

To Dad who always encouraged me to be a salesman and show there are no limits to how much you can sell!

To Mom, who when I was young, was so delighted with all the junk I brought home. She put up with the stuff I took apart to see how it was built (see an antique photo of her on the cover of this book, as a child).

My friend Mike, who has been a great teacher and example. He shared tips, stuff and experiences as a truly professional picker.

Thanks to all of the other pickers, colleagues, dealers, and customers who helped me, sold to me, and bought from me.

A special thanks goes to Dave Brimley who fashioned the cool sign you see on the book's cover and to Steve Tregeague who took the cover photograph.

I'm very thankful to Nick Pfeifer, a special, very talented young man who drew the cartoon illustrations used in this book.

# Preface

*What in the world is a picker? What does this have to do with antiques? What are all the secrets about?*

Do you find old things interesting and enjoy antiques? Do you know that there is a large sub-culture of hunters, foragers, and gatherers finding these things? These people, we will call "pickers," glean from the fields of trash and junk beautiful, valuable antiques and treasures. They are hard working and sometimes very clever experts, seeking and finding many types of interesting objects. They find rare and historically important items we see in museums and fine antique stores. These pickers not only find the rare, but many useful products as well. Some make a very good living doing this.

Secrets? Pickers, as we describe here, have been gathering and reselling used things as an occupation forever. Most of the population is not even aware of them. Even the sophisticated shoppers that spend so many dollars at antiques stores and collectibles malls hardly question where the items come from.

It is the pickers who find and rescue much of what would have been lost forever in the dump. It's the pickers that help drive the interest and market for emerging collectibles.

This book will tell you how and why it's happening. As an observer you will gain insight. As a participant, whether picker, collector, or as a dealer, it will assist you. There are wonderful tips, ideas, and techniques you can try immediately.

Probably today more than ever before, picking is a valid and worthwhile effort;

**Number one:** The economy is uncertain and is demanding us to find ways to supplement our incomes. For example, many pickers take on extra jobs, start small side businesses, or try to create other ways to receive extra income. When you go picking and then sell the items you find, it's like another job, having a small business, and a profitable form of investing.

**Number two:** The world is full, and others who have lived are passing on, causing their wealth and worldly goods to be re-distributed. Pickers discover these things and aid in this re-distribution of goods.

**Number three:** People now more than ever in the world's history have more choices of objects. New, improved, and amazing things they feel they must have because marketing tells them they do. But guess what? There's not enough room! So they sell, give, or donate the old stuff. This is good pickings for those with the knowledge and insight into the value of this disposed-of product. The secret is, that old stuff tends to have more lasting value than the new improved stuff. Early products were made in smaller quantities than the mass produced stuff of today. Limited availability drives prices up, you know. It's that supply and demand business. Besides, rare antique stuff when you find it, is really fun!

**Number four:** Baby boomers are at the peak of their nostalgia cycle. They remember their old toys and other items. They remember their parents and grandparents stuff. They need to have that item they haven't seen in years. After all, they'll never find another one again, so what if it's ten times its original price—it's worth it. Pickers know this and feel it too. The item jumps out at you, with its old lettering, heavy and well-built frame, or classic markings that give away the era.

**Number five:** Information is at its peak right now. You can find information on all subjects. There are specialists in all areas of interests. The Internet is an amazing resource of information and history on every subject. There are some wonderful shows on the television like Antiques Road Show or on FX Collectibles that really increase interest. There is a fervor in collecting, restoring, selling, and identifying. Pickers have more information on each and every type of product or item they seek or find.

**Number six:** Everything is collectible! It seems you can find a club or books on all subjects imaginable. You can specialize in anything. There are many places to find things in your area.

# Introduction

I need to explain to you how and why this book was written.

Throughout the book you will see discussions, tips, and topics. These items apply to **pickers, collectors,** and **dealers.** I almost combine and interchange the topics among all three viewpoints. I do this because I really believe that in most cases people who are involved in this work or hobby are some sort of combination of the three.

This book is about my experiences, the experiences and opinions of many others, and my philosophy mixed in with technique. I wrote most of this book on the fly (while it was happening). I saw, did, participated, and kept notes. I wrote about things that worked for me and also some failures. I also have shared many proven secrets, tips, and ideas. There are many great methods discussed here to look for, find, get, and sell treasures of all kinds.

A collector has to obtain things to collect. So the collector may go picking for items or buy from pickers and various dealers. He changes his interests occasionally, and sells off items becoming a dealer. The collector who knows the ins and outs of the business, will assemble the finest collection and save money doing it.

The picker finds things he usually sells to dealers and collectors for profit. He may start to collect some of his finds all the while growing, learning, and improving. He can become a collector, and because he is expert in his specialty, he becomes a dealer for some things while still picking for other dealers and collectors.

A dealer may find it necessary to continue to pick in order to be profitable. It may be that he/she just continues to have some great sources still available. (If you have a great fishing hole, you use it!) Hopefully, the dealer has some collecting fervor to keep them enthusiastic about the business. A dealer who understands collectors and their passions, can relate to them. The best dealers also know how pickers think, and know what is important to them, this is because they've been there. Besides, if she keeps her pickers happy, they will offer her the best products on a continuing basis.

Hopefully this will clear up some of the confusion. So just read, do, learn, and most of all have fun! You will be a better picker, collector, and dealer!

This has been a very difficult book to write. I've worked for years on this project. The subject matter isn't particularly very difficult. The secrets weren't too hard for me to tell. The biggest problem I've dealt with is how hard it is to break away from the actual picking!

It's fun, exciting, profitable, very educating, and full of adventure. But, of course, on the other hand, I could not have been able to write the book without the actual experience of picking and dealing.

# Chapter 1:

# Why Pick?

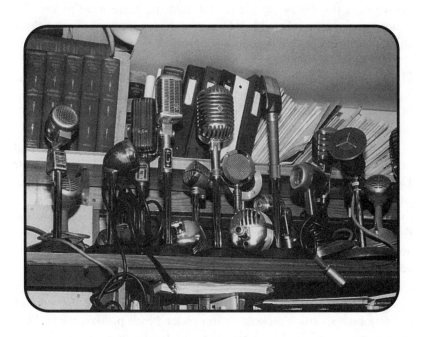

# Defining the Art: Pickers and Picking

The first time I ever heard about the term "pickers" was from a collector I know who had an entire basement filled with antique brass mining lamps. He also had walls loaded with miners' candlestick holders and other mining memorabilia. I asked him how he could possibly find so many fantastic pieces from around here. He laughed then continued to tell me of how he had pickers from all over the country send him pieces to buy. He said they went to places such as yard sales, antiques stores, and thrift shops looking for items to send him. He told me it was almost as if he had hired them to look for him. I had never heard of such a thing. I was intrigued and had to know more. He said that these pickers knew about this particular collectible and knew he would pay good prices for the better pieces. He told me there were pickers for almost any type of collectible. His pickers had a good captive customer (him) and he had an endless supply of good items.

The next time I heard the term "picker" I was waiting in line in a library book sale. The old timer in front of me was explaining how he had to get there early in order to get in front of all the book pickers. Here was that term again. He described how some of the big book dealers had hired pickers to find certain titles for them.

This amazes me. You mean that collectors, antique dealers, and bookstores buy from a group or subculture of people called pickers? Exactly. Just about anyone who wants to can go picking and then bring the items to these dealers and sell them at the back door. The fact is, the majority of the inventory that many dealers have originated from the front lines of picking. What you see in an antique store or a museum is an assemblage of items. It didn't just happen. It was built over many years of gathering, finding, trading, and collecting. It was all harvested.

Think of the word picking or "to pick." Have you ever said, "Look what I just picked up" or, "Boy, it was slim pickins today"? We've heard of berry pickers, stock pickers, cotton pickin', fruit pickers, rag pickers, even a miner's pick. These are all terms for harvesting, aren't they! Antiques and collectibles pickers are, in fact, harvesters!

My old-timer friend in line at the book sale spoke with a little resentment toward the pickers. What he didn't admit, was that even a collector such as himself was there to pick for himself.

Sometimes there is a perception that because something found its way to a thrift store or a yard sale it must be worthless, dirty, or just a doggy type of thing. The other perception is that if it is in an antique store it must be a rare and precious thing. I want to tell you that those

> ***"You mean that collectors, antique dealers, and bookstores buy from a group or subculture of people called pickers?"***

rare and precious things are found in dingy, dirty, and cluttered places and brought to light and rescued many times by the pickers.

The picker might be perceived by some as a dirty scrounger, however, the picker is an artist, and a professional. I know of all sorts of pickers. Some have excellent jobs and just pick part-time. Others are unemployed so they pick full-time. There are those who pick just to stay alive. Some are destitute and homeless, while others have stores and businesses.

I know of doctors, corporate officers, and other professionals who pick during their lunch hours—you don't need to quit your job.

There are also the obsessed collectors that just have to pick. Some are just fixer-uppers or do-it-yourselfers. Many pickers supplement their incomes by scouting for dealers. Some antiques dealers pick on the side whenever they have time.

Picking ought to be thought more of a profession, after all, it is more of an art than it is a labor. Good picking is a talent. Picking is a great hobby or even a vocation for some, as well as being a very lucrative business for others. It might be a pastime, a livelihood or sport. Whatever the individual's reason, it can be very enjoyable and fun. It's a blast!

## Packrat!

Are you one of those people who could be called a packrat? Do you save stuff because it might be valuable one day? Do you keep stuff because you never know when you might need it, love to rummage through grandma's attic or search thrift stores, old hardware, and junk stores for treasure? Do piles of junk look like a gold mine to you? Do you frequent swap meets and buy, trade, or even sell stuff often? Do you slam on your brakes, make U-turns, and park funny just because you saw a yard sale? Does your heart start to beat fast when you go to an estate sale or an auction?

Packrat

 *"The picker might be perceived by some as a dirty scrounger, however, the picker is an artist, and a professional."*

Did you know that there are people that actually make their living doing stuff like this! Have you ever bought an item for $5 and sold it the same day for $100! I have. Pickers do it all the time!

Have you wondered how in the world antique shops get so much stuff? Where do they find it all? Have you ever declared, "My grandmother had one of those!" Don't you wish you had it today?

Welcome to the world and realm of the professional picker!

The antiques and collectibles' market is absolutely exploding. People collect all kinds of things. They get sentimental and buy for the nostalgia. The growth is great because you have to realize the Baby Boomers, a large segment of society, is getting to that age right now where they go after the nostalgic and have the dollars to buy it! I've read recently that in 1996, in the United States, the antiques and collectibles' market was close to $7 billion and growing to $12 billion by 2001!

You are, can, and should be collecting and picking for antiques, collectibles, and stuff! This book contains secrets, tips, thoughts, and experiences that will really help you, guide you, and professionalize what you do.

When I was quite young, I remember going behind the neighborhood stores and businesses and finding lots of fun and interesting junk. I was young—you could get away with it, as, "Boys will be boys." In addition, the time was different. Now it seems that dumpster diving is reserved for people with sticks that look for aluminum cans or the truly despondent. When I did it, it was just fun. Picking is truly an honorable profession, even though you get some deals that may seem to be so unbelievable that it may look otherwise.

Picking has been kind of a natural thing for me for some reason. As a boy, I remember gathering old pop bottles and car batteries to trade in for cash. I used to take apart electronic and electrical products and sell the

 *"The more you prospect, the more you find."*

scrap copper. I've found old TVs and radios. I even remember selling an antique wind-up mantle clock to a dealer for $5!

I was always attracted to surplus and thrift stores. I'd talk to people about my hobby and the next thing you knew, they would bring something over to give me. I also collected stamps and coins as a child, which gave me a little organization and structure as a true collector.

I mentioned I used to go dumpster diving behind shopping centers. In a dumpster behind a neighborhood drugstore, I found store fixtures and displays that really looked cool in my room. I used to bring armfuls of half-full bottles of perfume demonstrators that I would give to my delighted mother. I'd get all sorts of little junk that pleased my friends and myself. Lots of good trade stock!

In a dumpster behind a gift distributor I found boxes of postcards and greeting cards. Down by the car wash they had a hill out back where they dumped out the stuff they vacuumed out from cars, and I remember finding many of quarters, nickels, dimes, jewelry, and stuff like old stock certificates.

I remember having neighbors let me go through piles of junk and garages of stuff just before they moved or when someone died, and I remember bringing home trinkets, antique clocks, and radios that I'd swap, sell, or take apart. We even had a guy my brother worked for who called up and said he needed to leave town because the mob was after him. He said we could have anything in the house we wanted!

Since my adult neighbors and friends knew I was interested in old keys, science, and electronics, when junk was thrown out, they threw it my way. Curbside spring cleaning piles used to be a lot better when I was a boy, too, as people tossed away their stuff.

I was indeed a picker, but just didn't know the activity had a name for it.

Later on in my life I really got interested in collecting rocks and minerals. I collected literally tons of material—even many museum quality specimens. I loved to go prospecting. I'm kind of an old miner.

Because I was a picker of sorts from early in my childhood it helped me to be a better prospector. When I immersed myself into collecting rocks and minerals as a young man, and did actual prospecting in the field. This earlier experience has made me a much better picker! I truly feel and think while I am out picking that I am on a field trip!

It was literally like hunting for and finding treasure. My early adventures in picking paid off. The excitement, the hoarding, and the organization of what I found made me a good prospector. As I worked on prospecting skills, I would research the literature—this paid off, as did leads and hunches. Friends were also very helpful. All of the digging, trying, and searching, taught me that if you think, work, want, keep going, and believe—it really pays off! The more you prospect, the more you find.

In rocks or junk or antiques, I realized that to find the treasure, you just have to dig a little bit more. Sometimes it's just a bit more in the same area and just inches away. You have to read the terrain and look for slight hints and tell-tale signs that are an indication of the valuable ore. You need to study all of the literature, watch for trends, and listen well!

All of this experience gave me what I really needed to be a more successful picker. The habits and experience, passion, belief and goals, combined with absolute interest and joy all develop what is called a "knack." You'll get a knack for it! After reading this book and trying the things described here, you will be way ahead in the profession of picking.

## Reminiscing About a Few Great Deals

At the first auction I ever attended, I was both impressed and fascinated and I blew it. Some optical grinders came up for bid, and I couldn't believe how quick the sale happened! It was over before I even discovered, "Hey, I want one of those!" If I remember correctly, there were six machines in the lot. They were very interesting pieces of equipment. You could take a pattern of any size and shape, and these grinders would copy the pattern grinding glass to the shape. They had a large diamond grinding wheel, and all of the fancy electronic controls to do a precise job. The entire lot was bid and sold for $60. After the auction, I searched for the winning bidder. I talked him into selling me one unit for $60, the amount he paid for the lot. I got it home, figured how it worked, and played with it for awhile. Ultimately, I sold the thing to a company that made glass holograms into jewelry for $1,100. This gave me the cash to go buy my first personal computer.

At another auction I bought a hot stamp printer for $25 (incidentally, this was also after the bid was purchased by someone else, and the fellow realized he didn't have a use for it). I sold the thing to a bookstore for $200 in cash, and $200 in trade. Since then, I have picked up and moved more of these machines.

Once I bought a large wood display case with sliding glass doors for $100. It also had four drawers under the doors. When I got the thing loaded up and home, I discovered the drawers were stuffed with electronic parts and products. I sold the contents of the drawers for $150!

One day I purchased two old, new-in-the-box electron tubes for $25 a piece. It so happened these were some very rare and sought-after audio tubes. I sold them three days later for $350 each. One week later, I took the profit I made from the tubes and bought a rare antique radio worth more than ten times that amount.

In a thrift store, I found several boxes (500 pieces per box) of small electronic parts. I knew where and how the parts were used, so I contacted a supplier who dealt in the same brand of parts. I ultimately traded the lot for a new 8mm camcorder. I was out a total of about $45.

## What Do You Think I Am, Anyway!

Just what do people and stores think pickers are? Well, it's rather like lawyers, used car salesmen, and auto mechanics. Either you are loved and appreciated, or you're despised. My hope by writing this book is to lift the perceived level of pickers. This is, after all, a full-time job and career for some. This could be a profession, too, if you are acting like a professional.

The picker does a service. The picker has rescued many very important and historic relics, antiques, artwork, and fine furniture. The picker supplies extremely large and lucrative fields with product to sell. The picker finds highly sought-after merchandise for those with needs and wants that would be impossible otherwise. Broken pieces are replaced. Lost volumes fill voids in sets of needed libraries. Historical information is assembled more completely and accurately because of the picker. Beautiful classic antiques find the proper destinations to those who now enjoy them. Value is added to otherwise useless junk. And, importantly, the proper recycling that is so vogue currently was perfected decades ago by the picker.

The picker makes his own good living and is not afraid to work hard. The picker can be an excellent resource and consultant with very in-depth knowledge on products, markets and trends. Why does the picker sometimes get a bad rap? (Or what can you as a picker do to clean up your act and get the respect you may deserve?)

*Q:* Aren't thrift stores, yard sales and swap meets kind of a grungy and somewhat dirty environment?

*A:* Don't worry about it! The professional steelworker, plumber, and even doctors and dentists work in and around stuff I'd have a hard time touching!

*Q:* What about rudeness? It seems as if pickers seem to push you out of the way when you're looking at something they are interested in. Some pickers are downright abusive.

*A:* Everybody try harder! Here's one I hear the most complaint about—some even knock you over if there is good stuff, and lots of competition. There is a lot of difference between grabbing and quickly picking something up. Stripping of shelves is mean. It is a bad idea many times economically, because you can be left with unsold junk yourself!

*Q:* What about early birds?

*A:* I have to admit, the early bird does get the good stuff. Just be cool, kind, and polite. If you're first in line don't be obnoxious. Being the early bird is one thing, but some people just wait around (especially thrift stores), almost living there. This gives pickers a bad name. The early bird gets a worm and moves on. If that bird is a vulture and circles until its prey is dead, it usually stinks too!

*Q:* What about snakes, cheats and thieves?

*A:* Don't do it. Be fair and honest—it will pay off. There are enough good deals out there for everyone. Enjoy the good deals when they come along, but don't make one if it doesn't exist by being dishonest!

*Q:* They are a bunch of cheapskates!

*A:* Well, the deal has to be profitable in order for anyone to buy it. The pickers see so much of the same product over and over, that they get a good feel for what something sells for. If someone tries to sell an item at retail price or higher, a good picker will either walk on past the item or at least try to inform the seller of what they know about the item they are trying to sell. It could be out of the kindness of your heart, which could find you a good friend and maybe contact. You might even find it turns into a form of negotiation, and you may just end up with it!

*Q:* What about competition? Isn't it pretty fierce?

*A:* There may be competitors out there, but that constant supply and demand thing is what creates this economy that is interested in what you find. Besides, there always seems to be a different interest and taste for every picker and dealer out there. The variety available is truly unbelievable. The abundance is also hard to believe once you are out there. Pickers buy from other pickers! Because of the different contacts and the different experiences we all have, the value varies considerably! You could buy an item at an antique store at their listed retail price because you know what a particular collector or another dealer will pay for it. It really depends on who and what you know!

*Q:* Don't dealers consider pickers just a necessary evil?

*A:* Not so! I know dealers that love to see their picker come in. They share in the excitement of the find, and profit greatly too. I have heard the term friend used often as pickers refer to their dealers. This whole thing is a win-win situation we are discussing anyway. I think the pickers that dealers dislike are the ones that come in their store never buying or selling, only looking at the prices so they can know what their finds might retail at. If you have a great relationship with your dealers, you have ready customers awaiting your find, and your inventory turns quickly. This means PROFIT!

## Respect?

Some pickers, I'm sure, generally feel they don't receive any respect. They might feel people think they are crazy. People may say "You are such a scrounger," call you a packrat or make other comments, but we absolutely love to laugh all the way to the bank. There are some guys at work that laugh when I told them what I found on a search. Then I'd see them or hear about a trip they made to one of my haunts when they didn't find anything. (They, of course, are believing you can go one time and find exactly what you are looking for.) Other times, among themselves they laugh about it, but then one might come up and say, "Hey, can you look for such and such an item when you're out scrounging?" (Oh, so now I'm a resource!)

I've had hundreds of dollars in my pocket or at times, very valuable merchandise in the trunk of my car that I found while on my lunch hour. I might never talk about it, or in a fit of excitement show one or two of my co-workers what I have. They might humor me or even joke behind my back, but I find the stuff they buy at full price and use all the time. I find stuff they wish they had; I find stuff they want and even buy from me and I buy at pennies on the dollar. Some just think I'm a scrounger, others consider it lucky—I just find it fun.

Some get flabbergasted looks on their faces when I hint at how many thousands and thousands of dollars I made the last year in selling my pickings; plus it seems I still have all my best stuff!

I make good money at this. It's interesting, and I learn a lot. I have a skill doing it, and it is a legal, honorable income. The potential is high and the opportunities are endless. I have an edge in certain contacts, knowledge, and experience that you cannot buy. (Exception: those who buy this book get some of that edge!)

I really feel more successful in life because I think success is not the destination or any one accomplishment, but the constant completing of many endless goals. This pursuit as a hobby, business, or avocation helps provide that. When I'm not doing a deal I feel as if I'm wasting my time.

## The Happy Picker

Pickers can come from all sorts of backgrounds, and have many reasons for picking. Fore example, some people pick:

*As Employment:* Some make their entire living from picking. It might be from desperation, lack of work, or preference. Several pickers I have spoken to don't want the regular "8 to 5."

*As a Hobby:* It might be that you are just a collector. I got into it as a money-making hobby. I actually started as just a way to improve my meager collection. I found a larger world inside with some very interesting opportunities. I still keep the finest pieces for my collection—that is, usually, until something better comes along. Some do it because they love the history and the antiquarian aspects of it all. It's always good to have historical information and experience. This is a big benefit to those who pick, just as a scientific and engineering background can help you identify valuable items in more obscure fields.

There are some who also consider what they do as an investment.

 *"The whole law economy is based upon supply (dealers) and demand (collectors)."*

They probably do much better than with the stock market, but as with any investment, you can still be stung and lose your shirt.

*As a Business:* This can be in the form of a dealer, a broker, a shop owner, or just wholesaling what you find to dealers and collectors. You could also include people with many years of experience, who do appraising and consulting.

I spoke to a dealer at a weekly fairground swap meet. Here they have some large buildings that house some of the swap meet dealers. It so happens that the dealers have a semi-permanent location for their store during most of the year. This swap meet is open for selling on weekends only.

As we spoke, I asked him about his operation. It ends up that this guy picks during the week, replenishes his stock, then sells all weekend. He estimated he cleared $80,000 a year last year!

I've met others making similar amounts, and dealers who say they hire part-time pickers who easily do $30,000 per year. He says they only go out on weekends to do so. He buys everything from them on Monday.

I know a smart picker businessman who does very well because of his hard work. He advertises in over thirty national publications, certain niche magazines that he targets with display ads and classified ads listing his wants, and has a toll-free number. He probably makes twice what I do in my real job. He also has a large warehouse space to hold and sort his finds. He will attend several trade shows during the year to sell, but more importantly to gain exposure. These shows are usually very esoteric and specific swap meets pertaining to his field. When he attends a show, he will buy and sell all the way there and all the way back as he drives with his product. He may only sell $2,000 out of his show booth, but pre-sell and deliver at the show $10,000. Another $10,000 may be sold on his drive to the show, or on his way back home, delivering pre-sold items to his good contacts.

*"Oh, this brings back memories,"*
*is the normal response. It's why*
*they have to own it. It's why*
*collectors collect. It's why*
*the things you pick for can*
*be sold."*

He will also sell many large lots of product to the Japanese buyers who come through on annual buying trips. They know him because of exposure through shows and from his advertising. Yes, his ads just say "WANTED," never "For sale," but they know he wants it for something—to sell it to someone else. This is very obvious to them. He says they don't bother stopping unless they can buy $10,000 lots of product. He feels that in the USA, we don't appreciate the classic, vintage items as much as the Asians do. Apparently so, because they pay a whole lot more for it!

It's not just an easy job. Although it can be very fun, in fact, so much fun you don't realize work is involved. There is stiff, aggressive and sometimes unfair competition. There's usually much driving. This eats up gasoline and puts wear and tear on your vehicle. There is a bunch of time used seeking, getting, sorting, cleaning, fixing, and selling.

We mentioned above some skills helpful to be more successful to you as you are picking. Other skills that can set you apart from the other folks include being a good listener or bargainer, loving to do research, and knowing where to find good information. Even just loving to shop helps you. If you are an artist, or have a good eye for beauty and aesthetics, you'll have a skill many don't have. If you love to fix things, and have certain craft skills, you may get more for the stuff you find. Remember, those who are goal-oriented always come out on top. Hopefully you'll also have some good business sense.

## Dealer or Collector? Make Up Your Mind!

Some might argue that you can't be a collector and a dealer at the same time. I disagree. True, if you have a hard time parting with the best items, you might not have the finest cash flow, but a dealer who also collects has a finer sense of what a collector wants. A collector who deals can constantly improve his or her collection. There are all kinds of fine lines between these terms. The ratio might be completely different for each individual, but a share of both I believe, is healthy. It's unhealthy for a dealer to resent all collectors because of their peculiarities or a collector to resent all dealers because of their money grubbing tendencies.

We collectors need to thank the dealers for the wonderful products they bring to the market. Otherwise we would have very little to collect. We dealers need to love the collectors, bless their hearts, for providing the demand for our products. The whole law economy is based upon supply (dealers) and demand (collectors). If you take all of the titles away, this whole thing is about finding, moving, studying, improving, discovering, enjoying, and investing.

I once had an ongoing argument with a dealer who refused to admit he collected anything for himself. He said everything was for sale. He always sold good items and expensive items. He was a successful businessman because he was very organized and made a beautiful display of his goods. As a collector, I didn't buy much from him. It was all money to him. I did buy many items from many other dealers that were also collectors. I think I did better because they would trade with me. By being collectors too, I guess I felt they could relate.

Recently, I've asked a few others—even large dealers—if they collect. It has been refreshing and interesting to find that many do. I also learn what their interests and passions are. Who knows, maybe just knowing this will help me in future deals with them!

## Nostalgia

I've mused about how I'd love to go back in time and get a load of old neat stuff. Or, how great it would be to live back then when all this stuff was the new technology. No way! Nostalgia was not then, it is now!

Think about this. You now live in a particular time that is way after the 1800s, 1920s, 1930s and so forth and have a greater vantage point than any from those or more particular times and lifestyles had. History is documented now. It only happened then, and the full picture could not be seen—even to those involved. In our particular point in history, we can use our own memory, gained knowledge, and experiences. We can see and appreciate the differences in design. We can follow the change of the many different products through history, seeing all of the evolution and change. I believe that there are as many important and wonderfully exciting discoveries looking back at the past, as there are going to be in the future. Nostalgia is big business. Look at all of the reproductions manufactured. There is much of the past reflected in decor, advertising, music and fashion. Art and architecture often show off the old lines. Pickers profit because of all of this interest.

"Oh, this brings back memories," is the normal response. It's why they have to own it. It's why collectors collect. It's why the things you pick for can be sold.

Time machines would be great, I guess, but maybe it would mess up our longing for those simpler times. For the longing adds romance, value, and appreciation that we love and respect. Some think they can recover or sustain the emotion they felt back then as they find old things.

## Perks and Fringe Benefits for Pickers

We've all seen the books, junk mail, and the articles and ads promising, "Buy at wholesale—20% to 40% off!" First of all, if you buy low and sell for a good profit, your income improves. Also, as you buy items for yourself at yard sale prices (typically a dime on the dollar), your standard of living is magnified. Now, if you buy at a very low price, and then trade it for its market price for an item you want or need, this also amplifies your dollar. This is better than the promises of buying wholesale!

Here are some good examples:

One day when talking to another picker, I found out he had some software I needed for my computer. I was able to buy this brand new normally $300 software package for $50. I even got a free upgrade from the manufacturer! I made a legitimate purchase, and saved $250.

I went to an industrial company for a liquidation sale they were having. I noticed a piece of test equipment that I was aware was originally expensive. I bought it for $25 and sold it a week later for $1200.

I was given a large oak cabinet that I thought would look very appropriate in an antique store. I took a photo of the cabinet into the first likely store, and the owner said she was interested. I hauled it over in a borrowed truck. She let me pick out anything in the store I wanted up to a value of $200. Kind of a little shopping spree! I picked out an item or two, one was marked $90. This item turned out to have a value of a couple hundred dollars more after I got it home and did some research on it!

It's wonderful to buy stuff at a penny or even a dime on the dollar! Almost as neat as selling things at ten to a hundred times what I paid for them!

I found a good book one day that I had intended to buy anyway. The retail price was $24.95. I bought it at a yard sale for $3. Did not my $3 equal the $24.95? Isn't this better than wholesale? Do I have an extra $22 to spend on something else? My smaller dollars are worth literally as much as someone's larger dollars! This is how I improve my standard of living. It's great! I love it!

## Lifestyles of the Rich and Lucky!

This book is about doubling your income or more. It's about raising your standard of living. You not only make more income in buying and selling at a great profit. You also have much more money up front! When you are out picking for items in your particular line of goods, you also find many items you can use! The prices you find these needed items for are way below the regular or list price. So if you buy a mountain bike for $15 or a $500 roof top evaporative cooler for $50 as I did, you're virtually living at a higher standard of living than your income would normally allow. One time I found a very nice McCullough chain saw for $25 (all it needed was for me to re-attach the pull start rope). I find useful tools, expensive scientific equipment, and furniture for my wife. I pursue all sorts of useful stuff out of my general seek list.

This is in addition to the extra living you are making now by picking! You are living beyond your means but staying ahead! Great stuff!

## Pickers Were the First Recyclers!

One of the great benefits of all of this effort is all of the recycling that is being done. It's been this way forever. Pickers, for years, have been rescuing items from being wasted, into items that are now cherished.

As you rescue items from the landfill, you are doing a great service not only to the recycling effort, but finding things that are valuable and interesting.

I've even heard stories of certain thrift shops setting up free zones where people can drop off certain items and others can take what they need. Things that can be used, like canning jars and certain other useful items. You also might check with your local waste disposal agency for items. I am aware of a municipal hazardous waste disposal site that has a free store set up. Here residents can drop off all of their left-over paint, and insecticides and chemicals for proper disposal. They have this store stocked with near-full or even new containers of these items. You can go in and take all of the stuff you might need for free. You can go in and pick up perfectly good bug spray, paint for your house, or other items without spending a penny!

## Don't Give Up!

Discouragement is a killer in this business. It's when you see another picker or collector hauling his armload out just before you arrive on the scene that can really be disheartening. Just about as bad, is not buying an item when you probably should have and returning later to find it's gone.

I had a bad experience once where I noticed a small obscure ad in the newspaper classifieds. It said "Old Victrola" $200 or best offer, and a phone number. I called, the daughter was there alone. She had no idea if it was sold yet. She described it as being about four feet high, all mahogany, with an inside lid that said Edison. It also had about thirty very thick records in the bottom cabinet. She said all it needed was a needle. The dad worked nights, and I couldn't call until tomorrow. It was late, but I asked if her mother would be home later and if it was okay to call even then. She agreed and I did. When talking to the mom, she said, "Sure come on over, it's still available." So I went over, and the mom was on a portable phone talking to the dad, and he's telling her how he had already agreed to sell it to a dealer who was picking it up tomorrow! Man, I hate it when that happens. I looked at the machine and it was flawless!

What you have to keep reminding yourself is:

1. You still have your money!
2. Other deals will definitely come your way.
3. This is proof that you're on the right track, a little late maybe, but on the right track, nonetheless.
4. You are learning. Besides, it's better than staying still.
5. Don't dwell on the bad deals. If you want, make a list of the stupid things you do, or the sour deals. Now you have a place to store

**$** *"Don't brag, keep it to yourself; you'll be better off."*

those stories and don't have to worry about them. After all, it makes great conversation! (Much like fishermens' stories, lies, and "the-one-that-got-away" experiences.)

You'll know when you are starting to do well at picking. First your neighbors will show some astonishment and jealousies often at some of the absolute luck you have in finding good stuff. You may even hear from a fellow picker, something like, "You know Ivan and I were talking, and we have to admit, you're finding an awful lot of good stuff. You are a pretty good picker." Your head starts to swell, etc., but you can get very discouraged even while at your best! How?

It's called "being in the right place at the wrong time!"

You'll know when it's going good. You have your favorite haunts to check out. You have a good schedule. You have found good stuff here before. Your system for quickly moving and eyeing the areas works perfectly, and you don't miss much. It works, it's proven.

Then it happens...in the hands of your competition (which could be a fellow picker, or just a common shopper), is the prize of the day! If you had started in that place when you entered the store that day, the item would have been yours! You may just want to sit right down on the floor and cry!

Truly great fishing stories for great fishermen, the ones that got away, or think of all the big sports heroes and their mighty defeats or the great salesmen who were a nickel too high in their price and lost the million dollar bid.

It just means, yes, you are on the right track, and finding good stuff. Your time will come to get it. Never quit!

## Loose Lips Sink Ships

Sometimes in states of excitement, I've bragged about what I've recently found and maybe where I found it, and even how much I paid for it. This can be very stupid.

I did this once to a fellow I was trading with (like product) at a specialized swap meet. I told him exuberantly where and how I found the particular piece he was trading for, and it only cost so much, blah, blah, blah. Now I see the guy go to that place we talked about all the time. I had never seen him there before that conversation. I wonder what he's been finding there when I'm not around!

I've especially been tempted in telling other pickers to keep an eye out for a certain pre-collectible for me. This happens to be a very good cash maker for me right now. No, don't tell! I can still find them, they are still only a dollar or two apiece instead of "list" price.

Don't brag, keep it to yourself; you'll be better off. If you simply have to say something to someone, find a confidant who won't stick you in the back.

## You Have "Arrived"

You know you have arrived when many times by surprise, you get leads to deals seemingly out of nowhere, but on a fairly regular occurrence. These leads come from friends, fellow workers, other collectors and pickers, and family. Or, you might just be talking to someone in a public place and someone sticks their head around the corner and includes himself in the conversation. He might say, "Oh, I have one of those," or "My aunt has a basement of them she wants to get rid of." It may be someone who, because you were talking antiques a month or a year ago, now needs your expert advise on how they can dispose of their family's estate that now needs liquidation. (I had five of these deals in the last year, no advertising or anything. They just knew I was interested in old stuff I collect and gather.)

## The Ethics of Picking

So, I found a good deal, I mean a really good deal. One of those once-in-a-lifetime or at least once-a-year-or-two deals. It was a very good price. Was I unethical?

For example, If I pay $5 for an item, and turn it over tomorrow for $200, I make a real nice profit. Unbelievable profit margin!

Did I take advantage of the seller? Did I take advantage of the person who pays me $200? Am I a terrible person?

Okay, these are some good questions. Let's look at some possible answers or at least try to rationalize, or you just might go crazy and maybe feel bad about what you are doing with all this stuff.

I go traveling in the desert and find a gold nugget. It's big, pure, and beautiful and feels heavy. It was put there by nature, and this is the first time man has ever seen the thing. It is a one-ounce beautiful, clean nugget. I paid nothing for it except for gasoline to get to the site.

This gold nugget has value. I didn't pay a penny for it. I could get close to $300 to $400 for it.

Did I take advantage of anyone? Should I pay someone for it? After all, it was found on public land. Should I give a large discount to the buyer because, after all, I didn't have to pay anything for it?

If someone gives me an antique and I go and sell it for $500, do I take advantage of the giver or the buyer? If I find that same antique in a thrift store or at an estate sale for $5 and sell it for the same $500, am I taking advantage of anyone? Is this immoral? Or am I just a good investor? (I really did buy something for $5 and sell it for $500! The buyer knew how much I paid for it, and was very pleased to pay the $500. To him, this was a bargain.

As a prospector, I studied literature on the terrain and looked for certain geologic features to find the gold nugget. I traveled the desert twenty or thirty times before to see if I could find the lode. As a picker, I also studied my specialty in the antique field, read books I paid money for, and I made several purchases before the big profitable find that were poor investments. This time and studying, along with the trial and error creates knowledge that has to count for something.

I invested money and time to learn about it.

I invested time to go find it.

I invested energy to get it.

I invested the funds to procure it.

I invested effort to clean, repair, restore and display it.

I invested study and time to find customers for it. I work to move it.

I invested experience and knowledge of how to find it.

I invested the risk, knowing full well it might not sell or might sell at a loss eventually.

This is an education we're talking about. It's years of experience, effort, study, and investment and risk. It is the same if you are a doctor, or contractor, or business professional, or a retail merchant. Your efforts must be worth it. The fee, bid, service charge, or profit is your pay for a job well done.

You see, I virtually went to school and paid good money for this education. I bought books, studied by talking to dealers, collectors, and professionals. These were my teachers and professors. Other school expenses include traveling, subscriptions, and an extremely high long distance bill. I put in the hours looking for, procuring, grading, comparing, pricing, cleaning, reading, repairing, and taking apart the things I find. The only way you can bill for these services is your profit made.

But what about the idea that you are making money off others' misfortunes? I mean an estate sale occurs because someone died. Many moving sales may happen because of a divorce. Isn't this a terrible thing to do? It used to really bother me to think about all of this.

One day I was helping a newly divorced lady out of her home. We were putting her belongings into a large trailer. The trailer was getting full with the items she really wanted to take. She also threw away many usable items. The largest and best of those she didn't want went to a local thrift store. Now I know the thrift store was not taking advantage of her. You see, the thrift store is a solution to this woman, as well as many others.

Doctors make their living from people who are sick. Lawyers depend on people who are in trouble to further their career. Firemen exist because of damage. Police, funeral directors and news people all do the same. You see, doctors are a solution for the pain. Lawyers correct and justify trouble. We all live and do the same. Humans are the only species who survive by serving others.

You are not stealing (at least I hope you're not) when you buy and clean out a deceased person's house. You're not vultures when you sort through some deceased person's belongings—you are a solution for the estate.

I found as I personally was involved as executor of my parents' estate, there was more stuff than our families had room for, let alone any future ability to use, so having an estate sale was not a violation in any way. This was a solution, a wonderful solution to us. You are doing a favor for the heirs. If you don't pick and buy, they throw or give it away—then it's just garbage.

When I finished with a big brokering deal I put together, I realized a lot about "stewardship" and "value added." I wondered about the pricing of the estate, the profit the dealer would make, and about my dealings. Was this all done correctly and honestly? I really believe if you are ethical, you'll do better in this business than those who aren't. Honesty pays off. The Golden Rule is still in effect. Making a profit is in itself not bad or wrong, but taking advantage of someone and stealing is bad.

So, what if the dealer bought a lot of stuff for $1,000 cash and ends up selling the lot for $2,000, or even $5,000? Is it OK to double the money, but not more? What if the seller names a price, but it's way below what the buyer was ready to pay?

You will find endless ethical questions in this business, or I guess in any business.

First let's touch on stewardship (more discussed later). When I have an item, it's my property, and I paid for it. I have stewardship. It's mine to use, dispose of, break, give away or sell. I have ownership and I have a responsibility of its use. If I sell it, my stewardship is gone. If I die, my stewardship passes to someone else. I can't do anything again with the item. I've had my turn.

If an estate has legal claim on the item, it is now their stewardship. If they turn the sale or disposal to someone, that person has stewardship. If I buy it, I get to play with it next—you can't take it with you.

Now let's talk about value added.

Let's take the items that sold for $1,000 we mentioned above. The worth or value at this time they were sold is $1,000. That's it; that is what the seller got, and therefore, is the value.

"But the seller could have received more if he would have asked for more?" This is true, but he didn't. For whatever reasons, decisions that were made during the transaction, side deals, pressures, thoughts, or feelings, the deal went for $1,000.

"But the dealer is going to make a $4,000 profit!"

This is true, but look at what is involved. (Think value added.)

The dealer has overhead.

The dealer or buyer may have to transport it across several states. This might require shipping or renting a truck, and spending money on removal, packing, and protecting. The dealer or buyer has to know about the stuff. He has spent years studying about it, reading, inspecting, gaining experience and knowledge.

The dealer or buyer has the contacts and ready customers he has built up over time. He may have to clean or repair it, or restore it by removing damaging modifications using products he has on hand. He/she may have to go into debt to finance this buy, spend hundreds of hours, pay for labor to process the items. (Is the seller having to spend the time?)

The dealer or buyer may have to buy the bad and unsalable items along with the good, catalog, sort, test the product, and advertise. He/she may have to take it to specialized shows or sales to dispose of it, place it in a store and display it, or even pay for a rental storage space to warehouse it until sold.

## Value-added Lesson

Think about this little observation as you consider how value grows: (Try and guess how many dollars per pound!)

1. Iron ore deposit.
2. Iron ore high-grade.
3. Cast iron ingot.
4. Rolled steel.
5. Knife.
6. Needles.
7. Surgical steel.
8. Spacecraft components.

We are talking about work and money. Just saying a dealer makes a hefty profit is not a complete statement. You knowing this will help. (It's also good to show this part of the book to your heirs regarding your future eventual passing). It is good instruction.

The value of something is what you can or will take the time, energy, and effort to sell it for. The value to another person is what they can sell it for!

As a seller, you have a lot of product to liquidate into cash. Here are the options:

1. Show it to a potential buyer who will take it all wholesale. (This is the quickest sale=10¢ on the dollar)
2. You can sort, fix, clean, display, price, and show it to many individuals at estate sales, yard sales, swap meets, etc.
   (A fairly quick sale except for your labors=25¢ on the dollar)
3. You could take it to various dealers at their businesses, taking particular lots they have interest in and wholesale it to them.
   (More time and money=50¢ on the dollar)
4. You can open a shop, display it, mail order it, and sell it to the public retail.

(This process is a very long sale, with lots of time and other expenses involved= full dollar)

## Challenges and Problems

Look at this list. Realize there are indeed pitfalls to this, as well as any new business. You need to understand these things, going in with your eyes open.

Bad checks
Bad credit
Bad deals or trades
Bad ideas
Bad investments
Bad leads and bad information
Bad stuff
Being taken advantage of
Breakage
Burn out, lack of interest
Business failure
Changed minds
Competition bought first
Competition sold to customer first
Debt and cash poor
Delay in buying
Disasters, fire, water, earthquake, damage.
Dishonesty
Fears
Getting scooped
Greed
Hi-grades vs. junk
Lack of knowledge on products, pricing, etc.
Overwhelmed
Poor decisions
Poor management
Shattered dreams & hopes
Shipping losses/damages
Stupidity
The economy
Theft, vandalism, burglary
Too late
Too little time
Too much stuff and no room
Unhappy, dissatisfied customers, and refunds

On the other hand, this can be an exciting and fun venture. You can be very successful. You can have a very rewarding and fulfilling experience.

## Sour Deals Happen

You get a call—the deal you made last week went bad. He wants his stuff back or money returned. The deal went south! Garbage! You feel bad, you're mad, you're worried, for now you may have cash problems. You have that yucky tight nauseous knot in the pit of your stomach. Stuff happens!

Sometimes you can re-negotiate. They train the soldiers that if they're ever taken prisoner, to escape as soon as they possibly can after capture, for their chances are better. If you quickly decide what the deal is worth to you at a lower level, you may be able to rescue it right now.

You may be able to throw in something extra to satisfy him. Hopefully as you keep talking, and realize what the problem is, you may find a solution that helps both of you.

Sometimes the person is one that doesn't listen to reason, and nothing you say or do makes a difference. Sometimes they may have a money problem, or spouse problem, or something else that prevents them from going on.

But, remember this: You will get over it.

You are smarter now (you will be more cautious in the future with this person). This is part of the picker education you are paying for. Your stuff still has the value it did before this deal. You'll sell it again. If it was your cash you got back, you at least still have the money! The next deal might even be better.

Climb right back on the horse when you fall off. Go work on a completely different deal. Hopefully this will turn out positively and put this one way behind you and in perspective.

Sometimes a knock on the side of your head like this really starts you thinking. Just as competition, it's a pain and you hate it and complain about it, but it makes you better and stronger. Overcoming a bad deal and turning it around, though painful, will make you better off than if you didn't have the experience.

Keep your cool, tell them what you think, but don't let anger overtake you. Don't burn your bridges. It's just stuff after all!

## Growing Pains

As you see the antique and collectibles market maturing, you see signs of growing pains. I've heard dealers complain recently of how bad it's getting with all of the buyers and collectors.

They require everything in new or in "box" condition.

They are too aware or savvy.

Let's turn it around...

It used to be more common to find better deals at thrift stores or from dealers at swap meets etc. Sellers are considered dealers and ask for higher prices. The dealers use price guides to price everything. The end result being that swap meets are turning into nomadic antique stores.

I was in an antiques store where the dealer used the old price guide with lower prices when he wanted to buy from you. He'd then offer you 1/2 of the listed price. He would then pull out the new price guide, with higher prices to price something you wanted to buy. He was pretty smooth about how he did it, and I'm sure most people didn't realize he did it. To me it was obvious.

## Quit Shooting Your Mouth Off!

It's poor form to brag. Besides, it can get you into trouble. You might give away your secrets! Other dangers are that you might reveal your customers, vendors, or profit margin. Some people who are constantly boasting also reveal a clue to their intelligence, which could backfire on them.

Sometimes you might have a great deal you pulled off, that has a fantastic story that you just have to tell. You end up finding that the story just upsets others, making them feel bad or jealous. Here you thought you were just impressing them!

## How to Get People to Constantly Keep Pestering You and Never Go Away!

If you have an item that you like and will probably keep for a long time, make sure you tell some interested people that you might, one day, sell it to them. They will bother you constantly. This will go on for months turning into years. They will never give up. Of course, if for some reason you wish they would leave you alone, say it's not for sale in the first place!

## Don't Waste Your Time On Him!

Once in awhile, you will encounter a real "bozo" in this business. They show great intentions toward buying something from you, or maybe selling something to you. Then they get real "flaky." They might tell you to call them back next week. You call back and they tell you to call the next week. This goes on for weeks and weeks and months. This can go on indefinitely. You get excited at first, then lose hope, then go up and down like a yo-yo. It drives you crazy.

Face it, they are wasting your time. They either don't have the money and wish they did or, if they were trying to sell something to you they just can't seem to part with the item. Somehow they might not have the social skills to explain their intentions. Scratch them off your list. Then you can pursue the next deal without the worry of them hanging out there.

This is different than the honest person who does take months and more to get the collection to sell to you or the honest person who is trying to put together the cash to buy from you. You need to have some insight and determine between the two types and realize whom you can work with. The "weird" ones get obvious after a short while.

Realize that there is always a good deal just around the corner. Most likely more good product to buy than you could possibly afford. Remember, if you are selling, there is always a good buyer available for quality product. So move on!

# He Was a Know-it-all, I Suppose That's Why I Trusted Him

When I started out in a certain area of picking books, I had an opportunity to buy a full set of Zane Gray books that still had their dust jackets on and in "unread" condition. They were bought many years ago and set on a bookshelf. I really wasn't into Zane Gray, nor did I have any idea of their popularity. I knew someone who would know. I met this old timer at several book fairs and felt comfortable with his expertise. Jake was a major Western Americana collector, so I asked his advise. I told him about the deal, and how the person said he'd sell them to me for three dollars apiece. Jake told me that's about all they were worth, at least that's what he'd pay for them, or maybe a little more.

I kind of put it off, as I saw no profit in the deal, and figured that I'd be better served putting my dollars in stuff I had interest in. Years later, and after I'd gained more experience, I saw several of the same editions, in worse shape sitting on a shelf in a bookstore between ten and fifteen times that offered price! The opportunity to buy them had long since gone. Old Jake I guess, was just trying to get a good deal, too. This folks, is how you get smarter!

# Put it on My Tab! (Ouch!)

One major problem with your local market is buddies. You might get into loads of good stuff, and might have friends and acquaintances that have similar interests. You can easily overload the local market and they can easily run out of cash! You might then find yourself running a tab on these folks. Pretty quickly you can find you have a list of people each owing you several hundred dollars!

Trust and friendship are just a part of the situation. Yes, you might find a few go south on you. You lose the stuff, the money and the friendship. (Yucchh!)

But then your cash flow gets strangled! When you are short of cash, you can't buy the good deals that come your way. This is very discouraging and dangerous. Dangerous, in that you are tempted to go into debt yourself to buy the deal that comes your way. The first problem is you borrow the cash (dependent on the cash your friend owes you). Then you may only get the cash from the friend in little amounts that you then spend away.

So you borrowed the money (because someone owes you that much) and buy some new items, and the person finally pays you back. You spend that money he pays you back, on a new deal that comes along, rather than paying the debt! (Yikes!)

So remember these things when dealing with your local market; don't pile it on your friends. Don't give credit. Trade, swap or barter if you need to. Sell to the folks who have the cash. Experiment outside of your area to find new customers. They will probably pay you higher prices too.

# Forgive the Debt

I had a situation where I let a person take some surplus electronic scrap that was loaded with gold-plated devices. He was to salvage the gold and take a percentage giving me a healthy profit. After he took the scrap we spoke several times. He had a few delays, due to health problems, and so I waited. Later on, he and I would talk, and he'd keep assuring me all was going well. His delays kept happening and eventually I got the hint; he ripped me off. This made me more upset. I called daily for weeks. He wouldn't return the call so I'd leave angry messages. Then I finally figured it out, "I will never resolve this, I will never get satisfaction." He was dishonest—I am the victim.

My mind needs some type of closure to things like this. I called one day and spoke to one of his children. The message went something like this, "I had some product your father was going to process for me. It had a value of several hundred dollars. I have been calling for weeks and weeks, you know that because you took some of the messages. I know he is not going to pay me or return the stuff. I know he's being dishonest with me. But, please tell him for me that I forgive the debt. This will be my last phone call, thank you."

It really helped. I could scratch his name and number off my list. I don't have to be upset anymore. I learned some marvelous lessons. It was a valuable experience. Besides, now there is no longer a victim.

## *Watch Out!*

I was in a thrift store awhile back, talking to a full-time professional picker I know. We were talking about some of his finds and methods, and an angry woman overheard our conversation. She immediately got angry with him and started spouting off on how he was a real creep. After all, he was there "stealing" all the good buys first, and then taking his finds out to the swap meet and tripling his money! I was really expecting to see her start swinging her purse, just like you see in the movies. He tried to defend himself, by explaining how it's his job, it's his living to do this. She wouldn't hear of it. Didn't she realize that the thrift store she respected so much was doing the exact same thing? They are a non-profit organization, that depends on items given to them... for free, and then they price it, and sell it to the public. (I'll bet you she has found a good deal more than once and profited from it). You meet all kinds!

# Chapter 2:

# The Philosophy of Picking

## Feast or Famine Syndrome

I call it a syndrome. It happens to the best of us. If you are careful and recognize that it's happening, you might be better off.

I've had days where it's been very slim pickins and all I see is junk. The problem is—I buy some of that junk. Stuff I wouldn't normally buy, except because I'm not finding anything, I feel I just have to buy something. I've also had days and opportunities where there is so much stuff and so many choices, it's overwhelming. I usually end up passing on many items I'd normally buy in a minute on a slow day. Feast and famine!

So, at one end of the spectrum you are wasting money, and at the other end you don't have enough money to buy all you want!

I think many of us need to be more selective. Be careful when there is famine to not piddle away all those needed dollars. It really adds up. If you can turn the dollars fast, selling all the small stuff quickly, then it's OK. If you are a good business operator and have plenty of money, you should be all right.

Some pickers have excellent cash control. Their inventory turns regularly, and they have promptly paying customers. They keep their cash flow in order, and have the dollars when they are needed to invest in opportunities.

Many pickers, however, seem to work "hand-to-mouth." They never have the cash to buy the good stuff when it's available. They use credit too much, or they dabble in the small stuff because the hi-end products are out of their league. Several just plain don't know how or where to sell their goods. Many people also try to keep too much stuff, rather than moving it on. They also make many bad buying decisions.

Especially when beginning in a new area of collectibles, be very selective. You may need to be much more selective than you want to be. Go for the known and sought after items. Select the best quality pieces.

Working hand-to-mouth at first has some side benefits. Somehow you get very creative. For example, you might pull some real good stunts in order to get something that you want. You might also be able to obtain cash almost magically, to help you buy something you really want. Other amazing feats include deals such as "three-way trades" to various collectors and dealers. You might also have brilliant inspiration of what to sell or whom to sell to, when you are in a more needful situation.

Experiences can become techniques to use later on, even when money isn't so tight. You can learn a great deal from the feast or famine syndrome.

 *"Experiences can become techniques to use later on, even when money isn't so tight. You can learn a great deal from the feast or famine syndrome."*

## Get Ready, Here it Comes!

Some days you will find more stuff than you can feasibly carry! There might be more than you can possibly pay for. There might be possibly more than you have room for. There might be more than you have time to go through. There may simply be more than you want.

Some options are:

1. Broker some of it.
2. Partner with someone for some of it.
3. High-grade some of the better pieces and walk away from the rest.
4. If you get it all, quickly wholesale some of it.

There may be days like this. It is always good to have the knowledge of values and potential customers, etc., because you have more choices.

It's interesting how stuff like this happens, and you walk away from stuff that on a slow day you would be knocking over someone else trying to grab. When it rains, it pours!

## Treasure Hunts:
## "The Pursuit is Better Than the Having"

Do you ever notice that there is more enjoyment in trying to get and then obtain an object, than there is in the actual owning of the object? It's sort of like Christmas. When the kids open the presents, the joy is the anticipation and the surprise. When it's all over, you never quite get back to that original "rush" of excitement. The child plays with the toys on Christmas Day, trying very hard to relive the sensation of getting, but it never comes close.

> *"First comes the excitement, which helps you have the energy to obtain an item, then the reward."*

Some pickers love the work because of the thrill of finding treasures. The enjoyment is up front. The next stage is just so much stuff. There is a satisfaction again upon the sale of the items, but nothing can beat that original exhilaration of uncovering a real jewel.

My wife asked me once a question that was very revealing, "Do you have more enjoyment in the collecting of stuff or in the having of it?"

It did not take me long to answer, "Collecting!" Whether it's picking or finding, hunting, scouting, searching and researching, purchasing, negotiating, scrounging, buying, dickering, trading or procuring—the adventure is here! It's just like sport fishing or hunting—your trophy is there usually just to remind you of the experience. There are still many mountains to climb, new places to check out, basements to be cleaned, boxes to be opened, people to talk to and things to find.

## Preaching About Wants

You'll have to bear with me while I do a bit of preaching. This is a product of my own understanding and rationalizing, but it is good information to help you know your seller and your customers as you start dealing. This whole business is based upon wants. You want, they want, we see, we like, we get, we show. Somehow we gather comfort from these worldly finite items.

It's all just stuff.

It's plastic, glass, metal, paint, and color.

It's inanimate, blind, and soulless.

Worth is brought about by talking and chattering about it. Value is only a perception. Price is an absolute illusion. It is pride of ownership that drives people to collect. It's having something more or before the other guy that gives us victory. We somehow feel more valuable by having it.

The drive, the passion, the obsession—all of the other stuff, whether historical, nostalgic, artful, important, or rare is only a rationalization. Compare your understanding of the topic above to the topic below. If you understand the above better, you will make it work better.

You may be making a full-time living owning a successful business, or just supplementing an income. You might just do this for fun, or to satisfy a need to collect. On the other hand, if you get too hung up on the things, it will be difficult to sell or trade. You need to let go in order to make a profit.

If you let go, if you sell, you will move and turn-over your inventory. You will have and find numerous more contacts and better items. You will grow. Hoarding ultimately hurts you. If, however you sell to others that hoard, it serves to fulfill their needs and insatiable wants while it helps you. The more you give, the more you get.

## Enthusiasm!

Enthusiasm in anything is an asset! Enthusiasm also goes in surges and stages.

You are on a hot trail. You just found out that a whole garage full of goodies is available. You just might have a chance to buy the entire lot at a good price. Better than that, no one else even knows it's for sale!

This first stage is euphoria. You may dream about it, that is, if you can sleep! You count your shekels; that is, you try to figure the profit you will realize if it goes through as you plan. You worry it might not happen. You worry about the competition finding out and out bidding you. You worry the seller will change their mind. You get "feelings" such as butterflies, sick pangs, and irritability.

The next stage is more controlled. Guess what, it is going to happen. Appointments are established, the dollars are discussed. Transportation and storage is arranged. It's yours! The deal is done.

The last stage is the possession, the victory. The euphoria and other physically felt emotions are gone. It's a controlled joy, or satisfaction. The stories can now be told. The travel and the quest in advance of obtaining are always more exciting than having the item. First comes the excitement, which helps you have the energy to obtain an item, then the reward.

Redistribute the wealth!

## Redistribute the Wealth

I went to an open house at a large church-run thrift store a couple of years ago. I heard a talk by an individual who was employed there as a trainer. You see, they not only sell stuff to help feed the poor, but they go much further. They have many functions. Besides a church welfare operation, they train the individuals to work in a variety of operations. They purposely turn over a large population of employees, providing the community with a group of trained, capable workers, who would normally be unable, unemployable people.

They provide the donations to the public at low prices, or bargains, realizing many people could not afford to buy at retail and need these products for their own use. They are well aware of the pickers and they refer to them as dealers. They understand that their store not only provides work and training for the individuals they employ, but provides a living to many others who sell the products found there. They consider their role is also to re-distribute the wealth. Seems like a worthy goal.

## Stewardship

What do you have? Do you really own it? Ownership, better described as stewardship, is how all this stuff we are doing works. If you want to be good in this business, you need to understand how steward-ship works. Very simply, someone makes something (or finds it in the earth). They hold onto it for awhile. They use it, keep it, sell it or give it away. They have it for awhile then someone else gets it.

I hate to remind you, but you are temporary. This stuff you have is temporarily yours. Absolute ownership of physical items is an impossi-bility. Humans like to put big fancy comforting terms or descriptions of ways to keep it, like estate, foundation, trust, or bequeath, etc. Some-how this keeps our name with the item forever. Um...not really.

Have you ever seen a gold coin that was made in ancient Rome? Do you know the name of the original owner? Do you have any idea at all about who the owner was one generation ago? How about all those other generations?

This coin's owners don't survive as long as it does, therefore, owner-ship is a poor term. Stewardship is more accurate, but stewardship also carries with it another component—responsibility.

We are stewards of things right now. The previous owners are forgot-ten, and all the subsequent owners are unknown. This is why we fix up, and protect stuff that is especially historical. It's not in just having the thing or it's dollar value. It's not just it's rarity or only about pride. It's about respect.

When you deal with historical, vintage, classic, and important valuable items, you are a temporary custodian, you do have some responsibility. Examples include:

*Protection:* You should have the proper storage area to keep any further damage from the elements, etc. You need to keep it safe from improper use, which includes poor restoration and cleaning (i.e. the damage caused by some antique dealers' favorite tool, the wire brush...ouch!). Is it insured while in your possession?

*Identification:* What if you found a one-of-a-kind or an important prototype? This is not only valuable monetarily, but valuable historically.

*Destination:* Does the important stuff go to museums or well-protected private collections? Do you deal with knowledgeable dealers?

You may have a variety of reasons for harvesting this stuff, just do it well! Discover it, collect it, identify it, appreciate it, enjoy it, and profit from it!

# Chapter 3:

# People and Pickers

## My Friend the Picker

I have a good friend whom I met through this picking business. As I started collecting and finding certain items, he was an illusive legend. "Oh, you collect those? You need to meet Ralph, he has tons of them. Everybody knows Ralph!"

Ralph was my big competition. He seemed to get everywhere first. If I was looking for something or answering an ad, Ralph had already been there somehow and found the prize.

I attended an auction seeking a certain item advertised in the classifieds. As I arrived, I quickly scanned the area, looking at all the possibilities and making notes. I waited for the lot I wanted to come up—finally it happened, "lot 54."

I made a bid then Ralph upped it. We went higher and higher until I finally got it. As I went to pay for it, Ralph came over to see who this other person was that was bidding against him. What a pleasant guy! We talked and told stories, I learned lots of good information. We became friends buying and selling from each other. I am much better for knowing Ralph, not only because of the insight and tips I've learned, but also because of his good friendship and attitude.

Ralph teaches and seems to be free with his ideas and techniques. I think he has learned that good old secret, "the more you give, the more you get." It seems to work for him. Ralph does real well when he goes out picking. He has a flexible work schedule, which helps him to get out on the best days, or anytime to find the good stuff. And he does find the good stuff. He's also very honest in his dealings with all the folks selling him stuff, and when he sells and makes his profit. All of his profits go to helping his family.

Ralph taught me how he looks in the paper at all of the ads, he marks the best possibilities and then goes to the library to find the reverse "city directory." Then he phones the people before the sale starts, to ask questions. This saves him lots of time out driving around. It also helps him prioritize his list so he gets there first. Many times he gets there a day early and buys it before the rest of the pickers are there. He really has a kind approach, so most people aren't offended. Once in awhile they hang up or tell him off. Some people really get angry at early birds. One good tip he discovered is that the city directory sometimes lists how long the phone number was assigned to an individual. This helps him determine how old the stuff might be in the house. If it shows the residence has been there for forty years, there is an excellent possibility for good antiques.

Ralph has a goal to go out early on his Friday and Saturday buying trips, and is usually finished before noon and home. After all, it really is

*"I have a good friend whom I met through this picking business. As I started collecting and finding certain items, he was an illusive legend. 'Oh, you collect those? You need to meet Ralph, he has tons of them. Everybody knows Ralph!'"*

all over for the most part after just a few hours. Usually, all that's left by then is the junk. As he hits all of his dealers, he wholesales to them on the way home. He sells an awful lot to them, usually having a good wallet of cash when he arrives home. Even with this, he fills up his double car garage several times a year with the stuff he has left.

He is always reporting how he buys things at very low prices and sells for surprisingly larger prices. For example, he found some antique country furniture cupboards he paid $15 a piece for and sold a couple of hours later for $375 each. Ralph says he can tell what items are worth by looking at the dealer's face when he brings them in!

He also taught me how you can usually find things at yard sales and garage sales that aren't for sale. At least they weren't planning on selling them before you came by. He always asks, "Do you have any old furniture?" and a list of other things he always looks for. He usually finds the best stuff this way. Other pickers and dealers can't understand how he can find so many good items. He is essentially going out to ask people door-to-door if they have any antiques for sale. This isn't done much now, but he does find a yard sale an open invitation to ask.

One time Ralph put an ad in the local classifieds to sell a group of collectibles he had just located. He said he doubled the contacts he had for these types of items. It was quite revealing! He said he feels there are many "closet" collectors, that don't surface until you bring them out. The small ad paid off in several ways.

*"Ralph says he can tell what items are worth by looking at the dealer's face when he brings them in!"*

Ralph stopped collecting years ago because he had a financial difficulty which forced him to give up his extensive collection. After that, he determined he would never get that close to things again. His wife is happy with this, and feels it's all junk anyway. She's happy with the cash. He considers himself a mercenary only in it for the money.

This has benefits, but it also hurts him in some ways. I've seen many pickers who work this way, and how they always seem to work hand to mouth. They usually sell off their find very quickly, and take a shorter profit just to take the quick doubling of their money. They feel pretty clever and satisfied with this, which is okay, I guess. But very rarely do I see any reinvesting or searching and waiting for the best realization of profit.

I have found many times that as I wait—especially on the very good items—I learn more about the market. I learn that the value in the price guide is very low for a certain item or I buy an item and months later see it in an antique magazine article. I need to let it age a bit sometimes, especially for the good stuff.

I know another fellow who, in the same marketplace does things completely different. He has a different specialty but he does, however, pick for some of the same items. He picks full-time.

Frank dropped out of the system because he was tired of working for others. He stops ten to twelve times each and every day picking for goods. He makes enough to support himself and get a few things he likes. Frank goes after what he practical stuff. He feels there is good money to be made in these items. His interest personally isn't in antiques, as there is too much competition, but the "50s" are interesting to him. There has been a recent craze for 50s period looks. He says he has been pretty successful in finding and selling many such items.

Frank warns how easy it is to go over budget on stuff. It is easy to find good deals and over buy. You have to remember you don't usually turn it over immediately. If you sit on the goods too long, you can get into a lot of trouble. He also warns of the horrible dishonesty that is in this business, "it's scary." He absolutely hates to see the mark-up that the dealer makes after he sells to them. This is what drives him towards wanting his own store.

After thinking over what Frank told me, I discovered something:

The dealer has to buy an item at a good price so he can make his profit. Let's say he has to buy an item for $70 and try and sell it for $100 (Frank doesn't like to see that $100 price tag). But realize that the dealer was not able to buy it for $10 like Frank did! Who gives up more? Let's break it down here:

| | | |
|---|---|---|
| "Fifties" Chair Bought at a thrift store for | $10 | |
| Retail Value | $100 | |
| Dealer Cost | $70 | |
| Thrift Store makes | $10 | gives up $90 |
| Picker makes | $60 | gives up $40 |
| Dealer makes | $30 | gives up $70 |

Now, this isn't always the spread, sometimes a savvy dealer makes a very large profit margin because he has a customer, or can sit on the inventory for awhile. Or he just has a better feel for the worth of the item, more so than the picker. But the rest of the equation is that the customer paid $100 for it! (He really pays.)

## Take it Off the Street

My best deals have always been "off the street" deals. In the sales profession, "taking it off the street" means to identify a piece of business, some potential big sale for a customer, and to work with him, give a quotation, and sell the product, before the competition ever has a chance to hear about it. The buy never went out for bid. The customer buys, receives, and consumes the material before anyone else has a chance of hearing about it. It is literally taken off the street.

This also works on buying material before your dealer friends ever hear about it. If you are searching the same places all the time (the same places all the other pickers are searching), the only thing you have on your side is timing.

To get an opportunity to take it off the street, you need to network. The way to network, is to let other folks, friends, and family know what you look for. They say or hear things, and it opens your exposure to many other opportunities to find what you are looking for.

You can buy things, before they were ever on sale. Your competitors don't even have a clue about it. Somehow you just seem to end up with lots of good material.

Don't be shy about what you are looking for. You can just tell them you "collect" (you don't need to say you pick or deal in the items). If you have a specialty, let others know about it. Show off your best pieces. Keep things on your desk. Tell friends and relatives what you do. They probably toss out or give away these things all the time.

## Pickers Have Pickers Too!

Yep, a picker can have a picker find items for the first picker.

I, being a picker and a collector and somewhat a dealer, have a few other pickers call me with their finds. They actually pick for me and I pick for some of them. It works out pretty well. The best arrangement is if your other picker would have never normally picked, nor is interested in picking what you go after. Otherwise they might sell to you at much higher prices, or be in direct competition. The best pickers are good friends or relatives, or someone you can trust. Those folks that understand your obsession will do you a good favor once in awhile.

**Tip:** The more you buy from these other pickers (and pay for) the more often you will get calls to see the stuff first. After all, they want to profit as quickly as they can on their finds too.

I have a good friend with different interests than mine. We have a good agreement. I find a few early paperback novels and some certain glassware items he goes for, and in turn, he finds me old radios. We also call each other giving each other good tips and leads, "Hey, did you see the batch of Carnival Ware that was just put out at ..."

You really have to know the other guy's stuff. For example, I was going to pick early mining lamps for a dealer, and he assured me he saw radios in various digs he went to. It happened that he brought me a bunch of old radios, but they were just a bunch of three and four year old junkers, not worth a dime a piece. It was hard to tell him the truth, after he invested his good money. (Although, I kind of think he made his money back when I sold him some mining lamps I picked for him....)

> *"It is easy to find good deals and over buy. You have to remember you don't usually turn it over immediately."*

## Wanna-bes

Wanna-bes are those poor souls who wish they could find good stuff. They are not true pickers and collectors. They hear of and see the fruits of real pickers and just think they have all the luck. These people are like those folks who like gambling. I'm sure they even read a treasure magazine once in awhile. While all along the jackpot and the gold is out there—they just don't realize how to get it.

These are the kind that have one piece of a collectible and bring it to you to see. You are kind and show some interest. You may even have some hopes of obtaining the item from them. Then they think because YOU have an interest or now want it, that it must be very valuable.

You might even offer an amount and they won't let go. You really don't care that much, for you might even have plenty of stock on the same item. You show them price guides and they get distrustful. After all, they have something you want, it must be a treasure. They will probably keep that thing forever either out of fear, hope, or pride; let them have it.

## Mentors and Apprentices

Find someone who doesn't mind sharing some of their knowledge and experience. Then you should remember the newcomer after you have gained more experience. The more you give the more you get... really! As you share knowledge you will both be better off. You get more, you get better, and it is a lot more fun than greed, jealousy, and bad feelings.

## The Competition

You will find lots of competition in this business. As you identify who they are, and what kind of competition they are, you have an edge.

*"The spoils of the battle are enjoyed more if there is a victory!"*

## Aggressive Competition

These are the people that can be the most troublesome. They know what you do and do it, too. They go after the exact same things you do. They know prices. They know the hot spots. They know all the players; that is, the buyers and sellers for the same things.

Note: these same people can also be your supplier. You might even buy from them. They may also be your customer! (Strange circles, huh!) The aggressive competition could also be good friends. Friends one day, and folks that would scoop you in a minute the next day!

## Passive Competition

They are the regular people, those who don't deal in, or might not even collect the items you look for. They just happen in and find an item and buy it. You might be going crazy trying to find the thing and they just haul it out to their car smiling.

You've heard that competition is good for you. I guess that is true. If there is someone else after the same item you are, that means there is demand. This helps the value of things. If you have to work harder to find and get stuff, you enjoy it more when you find it. This helps in satisfaction. If you figure out ways to do things better you are more successful. The spoils of the battle are enjoyed more if there is a victory!

## Networking

When you are looking around, whether it's an antique store, yard sale, or an estate sale, NETWORK. Talk to the other pickers, talk to dealers. Be friendly with the other shoppers. So much of the time we are afraid to talk, for fear that everybody is our competition. In a way they are, but in a way everybody is a resource too! You can gain so very much more by communicating and making good friends and contacts than by what you might lose at the one sale you are at right now. Everybody has different timing and places they travel to check out.

Everyone has ideas and "hunches" that are varied. Different pickers have varied interests, but their knowing what you like will benefit you in the end, as you now have more eyes and ears looking around for you. You'll be absolutely amazed what kind of network of good contacts you'll build, whether it's for tips or good leads or buying and selling to and from them.

## Missionary Work

Collecting or picking for certain items always goes better if you do missionary work. This means tell others why you are so excited about the stuff you do. You will be absolutely fascinated with what comes of it! My very best sources have been word of mouth, "Oh, you collect those? Well, we have an old...." And you buy with no competition breathing down your neck, and usually get a great price! You "take it off the street" that is. It never did hit the street, you bought it way before it ever sold to the public. These are the best estate sales too, those that never become estate sales. Everybody has something tucked away that's pretty neat. So talk up what you do, pass out cards, etc. You may not hear anything for months or even years, but one day out of the clear blue—wow!

Missionaries need to get good referrals. You need to spread the word and talk about the quest you are on. I've been amazed to find out how many people have an old antique item laying around down in the basement, perfect strangers, relatives, friends, everybody—either they do or they know somebody that does. I have bought several estates of stuff I collect just by saying I collect something to a friend. "Oh, then you need to call ....She has a whole basement of those she wants to sell."

You find more and better stuff this way. Usually just by a mere mention of my specialty. So speak up! Say what you are doing! Get referrals!

I hope you are going to have lots of room for all of the treasures you are going to find.

## Picking Vacations and Trips

When I travel, I like to visit all the different collectors and dealers and places I can to broaden my vision and find not only stuff, but information. I also like to ask questions of the pros (those who seem to be the best in their field or at least have good success). Ask if they will let you record their conversation, or videotape their collection, or photograph stuff they have. You can learn an awful lot by doing this. At the very least, you need to write down in your notes what went on and ideas you got after your visit. Often model numbers, prices, or tips can be valuable in the future.

I also love to trade when I'm on the road. You see different stuff in different areas, and what might be common in one area of the country, might be scarce somewhere else. So take a box of stuff, if you have room, for trading and selling. Also have cash with you, because you'll find good deals.

Here's one of the tips I found while on a trip that seems to work for someone I met. This picker has some business cards printed up that he immediately passes out when he arrives at a yard sale or an estate sale. It's one of those cards with too much information on it, very crowded, but lists lots of stuff he's interested in. It works because he gets shown things first off that might have been unnoticed. He also gets referrals and call backs, or the people even tell him of stuff in the house that they didn't put out on the sale. He even has a obnoxious bumper sticker that tells what he does, that I'm sure pays off if nothing else by starting some conversations.

I asked him how he became so successful in a particular area he specializes in. He said it's because he is the first person he is aware of that put classified ads in a national collectors' magazine spelling out how much he was willing to pay for certain models he wanted. He simply got them. Now others who want them go to him (for a higher price of course). If you do this, however, be prepared with the cash, and specialize very tightly or you'll get too many responses.

On your trip, one of the things you'll want to do is get the yellow pages and see where some of the likely stops might be. Some good headings to get you started are:

Antique Dealers
Auctioneers
Collectibles
Estates
Pawnbrokers
Second Hand Stores
Surplus and Salvage Merchandise
Swap Meets
Thrift Stores

I also double check several headings that are in my special scope of interest. If I don't have time or transportation to actually visit and check places out, I at least call a few places or people and ask questions. In your conversations, you'll learn an awful lot about the area, its collectors, and in addition, get good leads.

Ask who the active collectors are and where the locals find certain items. Ask about clubs, museums, or special collections. It is truly amazing to see how much information you get by a few simple questions. Once you get started you can really network quite deeply and find some super contacts. If you travel with some "trading stock" it really opens up doors too.

I have several times contacted people who actually pick me up from my hotel, drive me across town to their home to see their collection and let me purchase or trade items from their collections. You can find all sorts of treasures this way.

I also keep a directory of names that I gather from ads from everywhere and for everywhere. This is "just in case" I ever travel to these particular cities.

As I read an interesting classified ad, dealers ad, or brochure I put it in the directory. When I am fortunate to travel to that city, I have lots of people to phone, visit, or trade with. I always keep a journal of my contacts and visits too. It may have use in the future, and usually pays off.

Another valuable tool to expand your contacts is the huge resource on the Internet. The world wide web, and usenet groups are found on every subject imaginable. If you are not now involved in the Internet, do so.

## You Snooze... You Lose!

Here's one of those experiences where you can learn from another's mistakes (mine). I received a call from a fellow picker friend of mine about a "great score" he came across. He bought an entire collection of antique radios from someone. He said there were over 200 radios. As he started to describe and list the pieces, I got very excited. Then it happened...

I asked him if he'd tell me where it all came from. He told me who and how it happened. My heart sank. I could have easily had the opportunity weeks before if I'd been more astute. This was embarrassing. After all, I am the one who "wrote the book" on picking; I should know better!

Weeks before, I found an old jukebox at a thrift store that I thought I could turn for a quick profit. My very first call was to a collector who

You snooze... you lose.

was big on jukeboxes. Somewhere in the back of my mind I knew he had radios, but I wasn't thinking about radios at that moment, I just wanted to move the jukebox. I asked the collector if he'd be interested. He said "No, not right now. In fact, I'm kind of getting rid of them as I can, really trying to get out of the business..." Now here's where I should have asked, "So, are you going to get rid of the radios?..." But, I didn't. I just started calling others about the jukebox. After all, I was going to make a couple of bucks!

I missed my cue. Here's where I should have asked, "What else are you getting rid of?" or "What about all of the radios you have, are you selling them too?" I was so interested in selling my junk to him, I didn't even listen. I just went on my way.

So then I get this call, "Hey, guess what I just bought, a whole collection of antique radios and stuff...." He bought the collection for next to nothing, and it took him days to get it all home and piled up in his garage. There were classic transistor radios, crystal sets, old battery sets, and table radios. There were lots of console radios, speakers, and horns.

I know I could have easily had the entire collection if I'd been a bit more aware. In fact, as he tells the story, apparently several collectors and dealers were called to come over and see the collection, my friend was just the first to make it! My timing could have been perfect! I would have been there a couple of weeks before any were actually called.

The way I do things, however, is I try and make lemonade when I'm given lemons. So what did I do? I went over and bought some radios from my friend. I actually got some pretty good deals!

## The Once-in-a-lifetime Deal

The once-in-a-lifetime deal is the opportunity that every picker dreams of. It's the reason you can get the energy to get up early in the morning if you have to. It's the tight knot in the stomach as you get closer to check out a lead you followed up.

I've had several so far. I know of several other pickers and dealers who have had one or more once-in-a-lifetime deals. (Even though you have more than one, go ahead and call it once in a lifetime).

These are the deals where you can make thousands of dollars profit. These are the deals that the seasoned collectors, who may have collected for many years, have been waiting to get. They drool and dream about it, but never get close. These are the items found that have great rarity, or have historical importance and significance.

> "Don't be too quick to make a buck on the important stuff. If it's a big deal, make a big deal out of it!"

## Caution!

When you find a deal like we have described, you need to proceed slowly. You need to be very careful and study the market before you hurry and sell it. For example, my friend told me of an item he obtained, and started to try and sell.

He was visiting an antique showcase mall where he has a case of products for sale. The shop owner said he had a person in mind who wanted to sell an old phonograph. They gave the lead to my friend Mike.

Mike followed up on the referral and went to look at the old phonograph. It was much more than an old phonograph. This was like nothing he had ever seen before. What's interesting, is Mike delayed in checking out the lead and then put off buying the thing for quite awhile, pondering if he really thought he could move it. It was the seller that wouldn't leave it alone. He finally talked Mike into taking it for $100. They even delivered the item because Mike had no way to get it home. The thing was too big. This was a large "Chippendale" style, inlaid wood on burled walnut cabinet. It was very beautiful and filled with a giant mechanism. This unit might even be a one-of-a-kind.

The device was manufactured in Salt Lake City in the 1920s. The cabinet was in wonderful shape, and well taken care of for many years. Someone had removed all of the tubes, but otherwise, it looked fairly intact. The "Ordomatic" had a lower cabinet that included a radio and the most amazing phonograph contraption. It had a four-sided turntable that would rotate after each record was played. It would take a record that was stacked vertically on one side, and feed it into the side turntable. That record was then fed into the vertical turntable by a rotating coil the set of records was stacked in. Once the record on top was finished playing, the tone arm would lift, and the entire turntable would rotate, bringing the new selection to the top. The last record that played, would "pay off" into the coil on the other side, and get stacked with the other used selections.

Was this a radio? Or a phonograph? Could it have been one of the earliest attempts at a juke box? Or was it pre-juke box?

Mike did minimal research and found a fellow out of state who advertised for similar items and called. This potential buyer asked the price Mike wanted to sell the unit. Mike literally pulled a number out of the air and blurted out $3,000 confidently. Now, what was the first hint, was the dealer was not even phased with this seemingly large amount. He said to Mike, just send some photographs and I'll send a "moving company" to collect the item and bring it to me.

After hearing this story, I challenged his attempt to sell this important item so soon. First of all, he only has $100 invested. Next, he doesn't even know what the thing is. I told him he probably needs to speak to some people in the associated markets, like juke box collectors, or phonograph collectors, not just radio people. I said I'd probably want to sit on it for awhile, and take the time to identify the thing. Then research the market and the people. This way he won't be leaving a lot of money on the table and enjoy some more profit on the item.

Now, usually, those who try and squeeze every penny out of their finds suffer somewhat. Part of the problem is that you may gain a bad reputation of not being fair to deal with. You also need to realize that it takes much more time to study and sell every item you get for top dollar. This is disastrous to your cash flow.

In the case of single, one time important discoveries, however, you need to move slowly. You'll need to find out more information, and find the right buyer at the right price. The temptation to make that $2,900 profit is pretty great. But what if you were able to make twice or more if you just added a few hours research and a few good phone calls. Maybe a well-written and well-placed advertisement would do it. It would take many more hours and much more work and effort to make that much on your money, doing lots of $10 or even $100 deals. Don't be too quick to make a buck on the important stuff. If it's a big deal, make a big deal out of it!

## He Has a Reputation to Keep

I was speaking with a dealer who has a large sales space at our local swap meet. He brought up a point that I feel is good to cover.

He mentioned a local picker we both know very well. This picker has a reputation for selling "cheap." He sells just about everything he gets and has learned how turn over is important. He makes a profit on everything he sells, but there is this perception he sells too cheap.

What happens, is that once you buy from him and get a good deal, you feel you are entitled to always buy at such a good deal from him. He couldn't get list price on anything from people who buy from him regularly. You want to move as much product as you can and be well-known. You don't mind wholesaling, but you want to make a good profit on the big stuff too.

How can you do both?

You are more anonymous if you sell some items in an antique show-case mall. You might try moving the rare and expensive items out of state. Be patient on the important and expensive pieces—if they want it, they'll pay. Try running an ad in the classifieds, you'll meet new people.

## Weird Experiences

This is a true story. I did change a few common things in the description to keep the privacy of the family involved.

I saw an ad for an estate sale. The description said that there was a large amount of the type of industrial equipment that I look for. I called to find out that the family was disposing of their recently deceased father's property. She started to list off some of the items over the phone. I started to get pretty excited with some of the descriptions, brands, and model numbers! We made an appointment. I went to the place, a couple of towns away, and found a very large, nice home in a beautiful part of town. As I started toward the porch, I decided something wasn't quite right. The house smelled bad. I thought, oh dear, they weren't too "clean" here. As I went into the house, I saw lots and loads of the items she described piled everywhere. I noticed much more than she described over the phone.

I hated the smell. I noticed that there was cat hair everywhere, and that the dad must have smoked. Truth was, this was the smelliest, messiest existence I have ever been in. But I kept looking as the lure of all the items pulled me on, even though they were dirty and had a "film" on them. I asked for prices on some of the items. "Oh, $5." I thought, "What! $5! Boy that's cheap!" She just wanted to get rid of it. Well, I thought, "Hey, I can clean this stuff up." So I started loading all the best, most expensive items into my car and paid her a very small amount, washed my hands in the snow, and went home.

*"Could have, should have, would have... you know the rest."*

I arrived home, got out my spray cleaner and rags, and cleaned off the outside surfaces—it looked pretty good. I went in and took a shower. Later on, I was out in my shop when I noticed that this stuff still smells bad.

My curiosity was getting to me. I called the daughter and asked, "So tell me, just how many cats did your father have?" She asked, "Why do you ask?" I replied, "Well, I've been trying to clean this stuff up and it still smells like cats, smoke, and well, basically really bad." She said, "He had five cats, but they were locked in the house for over two weeks." I said, "Do you mean that... your dad maybe died in there and you didn't find him for two weeks?" She said, "Yeah... yeah, that's right. By the way, if you take a little ammonia the stuff cleans up pretty good."

You'll find all sorts of experiences out there. I understand this happens occasionally even in the best of families. By the way, I sold every item quickly to collectors and made several hundreds of dollars on the deal.

## You Win Some and Lose Some

Here's a real life story to learn from. You get a call from a fellow picker. (Yes, you work with other pickers, or network, buying and selling to or from anyone!) He has a couple of items in your field of interest that are new, and currently sell for $300 apiece. He wants to sell them to you for $150 each. You hem and haw, saying you'll check around to see if you can move them. It is just a commodity market, that is finding buyers and sellers. So you call your contacts or anyone who comes to mind and find limited interest.

You call back now less excited, because you don't have an immediate sale for the items, but know they do have value. So now you offer a much lower price, say $50 each for them because, "You think you might be able to move them one of these days." He says he'll see what he might do elsewhere.

The next day calls come back from your previous inquiries. Someone told someone else who now really wants one. You could have made a good profit, had you known. You call your supplier back, and they're sold, for $75 each. Gosh, you'd have paid that much! Could have, should have, would have... you know the rest.

Guess what you just did? You just paid for tuition. Yes, just exactly like if you were going to college. It is tuition in the field you are pursuing. It's tuition in the art of negotiations. This is how you learn the business. You learn prices, what is a good deal, when is a good deal, etc. (hindsight). Congratulations, you're in the thick of it!

# Chapter 4:

# Places and Haunts

Use this as a list to get you thinking and give you ideas on who to buy from and sell to.

**Second-hand/Thrift Stores.** These can range from the tiny converted house or small strip mall shop to the large almost department store variety. They usually exist from donations of used, no longer wanted items. Some have a relationship with certain worthy causes, such as church welfare or veterans or handicapped organizations. The profits can be used to provide relief, to help train and motivate, to feed, cure, etc. The stores are usually non-profit in nature. There are some smaller thrift stores that exist as profitable ventures to their owners, and the crazy thing is, that they still receive donations!

**Antique and Collectibles Stores. Antiques dealers.** These are shops filled with the business owner's own inventory. They usually specialize in certain areas in which they have expertise. Many carry a range of products from small to large high-end pieces. Some may have a few pieces on consignment from some individuals.

**Antique Malls.** These are antiques stores that feature booths and cases filled with numerous individuals' consigned goods for sale. Some have hundreds of "dealers" with a multitude of specialties throughout the store. Usually anything goes! Antiques, collectibles, books, toys, and stuff of all kinds can be found. Here lies a wonderful education. You can learn an awful lot by perusing these stores. Take notes on prices, models, and items that seem popular. Usually the dealers using the cases or booths pay a monthly rent and a percentage of the sale to the store. Remember to ask about discounts. Some dealers keep on file a list of the discounts given by type of product sold. This lets the store owner do a little bit of negotiating for bargain hunters.

**Pawn Shops.** You might just be able to find a few prizes here. I personally haven't found much at these stores. It seems that the prices are quite high on many items. Even higher than at antique stores and malls. Besides, you have to make your way through all of the guns, guitars, jack hammers, socket wrenches, and big carpeted speakers to find anything. But, there are things to be found if you look far enough. Some people who get in good with the shop owners get great bargains.

**Auctions.** These are great, if you really want to get your blood pumping! Here you find the best items and the worst competition. But the best thing is they all want it for the lowest price they can get. You can get extremely good deals, or you might bid out of sight. You need to thoroughly know your item, it's condition, and current values. You must have a firm limit in mind before you bid. What an experience!

There might be a few prizes here!

**Flea Markets and Swap Meets.** This can be your local, every week-end meet, or in conjunction with a show somewhere. Your local swap meet is usually an "anything goes" situation. The swap meet at a show of course has a limited scope, with specialized types of materials. There are also certain regional flea markets and meets that encompass acres of land and take days to see it all. These large meets are unbelievable. You can find most anything you want. Because of the immense volume of prod-ucts brought, and the enormous competition, prices are kept low.

Always remember to save out some money for the last day, as the prices drop sharply for product that hasn't sold. Prices are not always rock-bottom at a swap meet. After all, most merchandise was purchased "out picking" and brought here to sell. However, sometimes you can find amazing deals at each meet you attend. Not everyone knows all of the market values of good stuff. Some of the sellers have a specialty and a good selection, which is better than random yard sales.

**Clubs and Shows.** A show can be a very enjoyable, educational, and profitable experience. This is where everybody comes out. The biggest dealers have booths selling the best products. You also see on display the best of the best items. Stories are shared and information is gathered. You can gain much knowledge and association in these events. People are enthusiastic, "pumped up", and ready to buy, sell, and trade.

The hype and fun and excitement is all part of the experience. Some-times a club breathes interest in your topic, which helps the economy grow for your items. (Hype+Fervor=Value!) You not only make good deals, but you can make very valuable friends and contacts at good club shows. If you don't have a local club or show for your special products, you could start one yourself! I know of an aggressive picker who did just that, he formed a club so he can move the stuff he picks over the months. Wise move!

**Garage Sales.** (Also called a yard sale, tag sale, or even moving and divorce sales.) This is about individuals selling unwanted stuff they have organized to put out in hopes to dispose of and try to get a little cash. Most of the time, this is not your best place to spend a lot of effort. Lots of clothing and junk is put out. There are exceptions and some wonder-ful surprises. If they advertise something in your specialty or if you are on your way somewhere, it might surprise you what you might find. One man's trash...

**Estate Sales.** Usually estate sales are the best of the lot. Here is where you can find good antiques and collectible treasures. Usually the family is by now in the mood to just dispose of stuff. The problem is the stiff competition at these sales. If the sale is well-advertised, you'll see a good-sized line of pickers, dealers, and collectors out waiting to be allowed inside. This is probably the number one source for fine collectors items that dealers have in their booths, cases, and shops.

**Surplus Stores.** These can be various types of stores, surplus, army/navy, electronics, or otherwise. You might find some good bargains at these stores. Usually great places to "poke around", because stuff is usually piled randomly and obscured by other junk and packaging. Also many universities have some surplus stores that sell to the public. You can find anything from file cabinets to scientific equipment. You might even have a local state or federal or military surplus agency nearby that you should check out. Often they hold large auctions where you can find interesting and valuable merchandise.

**Freight Damaged Outlets.** These usually handle newer products. Stuff that may have been bought in "lot" quantities by brokers. They are good to check out occasionally and be familiar with. You may be able to sell some of these items to people you see advertising what they want in certain classified ads.

**Salvage Yards.** Some cities have salvage operations that harvest windows, doors and all sorts of architectural treasures from home and building demolition. You never know what you might find here. They may also be a good customer for any antique building hardware you come across. Ask them what types of things they look for and how much they pay.

**Factories and Local Manufacturers.** Some manufacturers have surplus items for sale. These could be parts, finished units, demounits, defects, or testing and inspection equipment. An example could be a semiconductor manufacturer that occasionally disposes of a group of inspection microscopes. I've been involved in similar deals, which have been very profitable. They also occasionally have office furnishings and supplies. Many times the employees get first dibs, but call and ask.

**Collectors.** Always try and make contact with as many collectors as you can. These are good sources for product as well as great customers. As you get familiar with their specialties, interests, and wants and they with yours, you can make some good deals and trades.

**Book Fairs, Library Sales, Book Stores.** Find out when and where all of the good used book sales are. If you pick for anything in particular, there are usually books written on your subject, and you should also pick for them. After all, the collectors want the books, too. Some libraries have "friends" sales to dispose of excess and duplicate books. You need to always ask if they have a preview sale for members, and find out how to become a member if they do. The preview sale is where all of the good stuff is. Note: volunteers and employees probably have a preview before anyone. Many used book stores are also places to find a treasure or two. They can't possibly know the value of every book, especially in obscure markets that you may have.

**Other Sources...and Places to Sell.** There are many places and people to sell to, for example, museums, other pickers, dealers, friends, relatives, fellow employees, neighbors, etc. Ask around, tell people what you do. Get the word out and do some good networking. That word of mouth stuff is your very best tool sometimes. Some of the best once-in-a-lifetime deals come from friends. Word of mouth is how you find those pre-estate sales and private collections. These are all without competition and with better prices and often friends and relatives give you stuff.

**National Sources.** Get familiar with dealers who advertise nationally. Send for catalogs, in fact, get on all kinds of mailing lists. Look forward to certain types of junk mail. Peruse and study different types of information sent to be familiar with all sorts of products. Start collecting catalogs (especially old vintage catalogs) as you come across them. Be aware of parts and service sources.

**Magazines and Classifieds.** Magazines, especially those that cover your particular specialty can be valuable sources of information. You can gain a great education and working knowledge of your topic by reading every month. You can also harvest countless great contacts from these. Remember to circle those little bingo cards to get lots of information sent to you.

**The Internet.** This subject is way too big to discuss here. But by all means get on the Internet. You can bid on anything you wish to buy, or you can sell almost anything you can get on the auction services such as ebay (www.ebay.com) or (collectit.net). You can search and advertise on usenet groups. You can get on certain email mailing lists for just about any topic. You should bookmark as many applicable web pages and find as many links as you can to pages relating to your specialty. Learn how to use search engines. You can also design and post your own web page to market your products and to find stuff. The list goes on and on. If you don't have a clue of what I describe here, go find out! Get a good book or go to a class, and then try it.

Business is booming on the Internet.

## Antique Stores

The traditional store is a company that is owned by an individual or persons that own most of the inventory displayed. One of the hottest phenomenon to happen is the showcase mall. These can be called malls even if they are smaller shops. These showcase malls have many display cases and booths that are filled with consigned inventory owned by small dealers, pickers, collectors, and others trying to move some products. Sometimes even other antique stores put cases in other areas trying to get more exposure for their items.

This all makes a very interesting display of product. The variety is usually very diverse. These stores almost create an historical museum of sorts. This is because each dealer usually specializes in his or her own, certain type of products in each case. The big difference between this and a museum is that this stuff is for sale!

It's a great education to go through these stores learning about products and pricing. You'll be astounded at how many items you will see for sale that you passed up while out picking. Remember, however, just because it's for sale and has a healthy price on it, doesn't mean anyone will ever buy it.

Here's how I work an antique store:

I am usually pretty focused on what I search for and collect. I have many interests and areas of expertise. This list is narrow enough that I can sort those items from the many thousands found in a typical store.

I quickly scan sections and shelves and rooms and move on. This is particularly helpful when you are trying to see many stores. Some towns have concentrated antique store shopping areas. To see very much, you need to look quickly.

Certain areas such as my collectibles or books or smalls slow me down. Many areas (even entire stores) I can quickly skip because I see they are not in my realm. (This is probably because I am just not informed or educated on the items.)

I go in with the attitude, "I'm going to learn something here today." I usually do and keep good notes of the visit. I also pick up any business cards, because new contacts are part of the learning I'm seeking. If the dealer has a certain expertise or specialty, it's noted on the card. It's always good to stop and talk to people, and dealers and learn what you can. The big opportunity is seeing how much things cost. It's also good to see how things are displayed and learn the merchandising techniques used to sell products. Make notes of displays that catch your eye.

I have picked up great deals even in the high-priced stores. You can even find thrift store prices occasionally, because of a less-informed dealer. If it's something I know very well, and it's priced right (and if I can afford it at the time) I grab the item. If the store has rented spaces or showcases, I'll inquire about rental fees and commissions while I'm there. Many have a waiting list of dealers wanting showcase space.

If you visit a store frequently, you can usually establish a pattern of certain cases and shelves and booths you like to check out. Some stores I visit have a well worn path I've left, as I zoom through the store.

## Estate Sales

If you are fortunate, you can get on want lists or preferred customer lists with estate sales companies. Some on the preferred customer lists get very good treatment, having a preview sale invitation. This means you arrive the day before the public does, therefore getting a better chance to get premium items. I've even attended these special preview events where they served fruit, crackers, brie cheese, and drinks to the shoppers. Pretty fancy! Having a preview means that when you go to the sale as the general public, you might be too late for the real good stuff. You need to buy stuff at these sales to get on and keep on the invite list. They do this for buying and spending customers!

## Real "Estate Sale" Lore

No, this isn't about selling houses. It's some stories that contain good information that you might find helpful when dealing with estate sales. These examples show what can happen before you get to a sale. (This is why pre-estate sale opportunities can be so good).

My first example is from a fellow I used to work with. He related this story to me before I got real interested in picking. He told me of how they cleaned out his folks home in order to get ready for an estate sale. They actually had a large commercial dumpster hauled in and tossed out enough stuff to completely fill it. He mentioned that there was a large amount of actual garbage. As he described what he tossed, we then supposed there were hundreds of collectible items. He said there were lots of old books the family had no interest in. There was lots of old toys and figurines and glassware. He also said that the day of the sale people were fighting each other to buy stuff "just like some of the stuff we threw away!" He had no idea.

 *"Never leave a pile of stuff alone or it might be grabbed. After all, you saw a bargain, it's likely someone else will also see it as a great deal."*

These things must happen all the time. Another person I work with, several years later, did something similar. They did some cleaning up before their folks' sale. The worst of it is, she didn't bother to tell anyone about the sale at work. After it was over, she told me of the experience! She said her father had an entire workshop in the basement. They took a few of the new, usable tools. They then invited the neighbor to come over and take anything he wanted.

Her father was a tile worker for many years. He had stored in his basement, boxes and boxes of brand new but vintage embossed ceiling tiles—you know the type that has all that filigree decoration you see in old turn-of-the-century buildings. They tossed it all out thinking it was just old junk. I can't imagine what a replacement antique hardware company sells them for or how much they will pay for them!)

A picker I know, who is very aggressive, astute, and proudly professes twenty-five years of experience in the business often tells a story. He spoke of an experience he had at an estate sale where he noticed out in the back yard a pile of about forty black garbage bags. Surely this was the stuff they cleaned up before the sale. He politely asked if he could go through the bags if he promised to not leave a mess. They said, "Fine, but while you are at it, look for something we must have thrown away by mistake." It was a piece off of an antique they showed him that one of the family members wanted.

As he searched through all of the junk, he said he found lots of old vintage windup toys, and jewelry, and badges, and many other collectibles. He filled up four boxes of good stuff. He also found the missing item that the family was looking for! When it was all over he wholesaled the entire lot for $350 to a dealer! You need to now realize that the dealer sold that garbage for at least twice or possibly a lot higher than he paid for it. He says he's sure this happens at most of the estate sales. In fact, he says he's had similar finds in the trash, many times since. Thousands of fine collectibles are tossed out in the trash every day. *Another mans' trash…*

## Sneaky Ways to Find Them

Here is a major secret that can give you an edge on the competition, save you gobs of time and gas money, and get you there first. Most of the time, estate sales and yard sales listed in the paper will list a short description to draw interest. They usually list the date and time of the sale and the address. They seldom list a phone number.

Here's what you do. Study the paper, highlighting all the potential good sales you want to visit. Go to your library the evening before the sale and find the City Directory. The City Directory is a large, backwards telephone book. You can look up an address and find a phone number and name. Or if you have a phone number only, you can find the address and name. This is a great book! (The Internet now has such directories. You may be able to look these numbers up at home or in your office).

Now, importantly, with care and tact, call the people and ask about the estate sale. If you are looking for something in particular, just ask. Most will be overwhelmed at how you could find their phone number, but just be nice. Tell them you have access to a special directory. Apologize if they get upset.

Most of the time you can get a better description of the sale and what will be there. You might even get good descriptions, model numbers and prices on stuff they are selling. Rarely, you might even find someone who will let you come in early, maybe the evening before the sale. If they have something you really want, I've even had them hold the item for me.

This way of making an early contact can save you lots of time and energy trying to check all the stops. Plus you can prioritize your highlighted stops, or remove some completely.

## Estate Sale Secrets

If an estate sale is on a Friday and Saturday, sometimes you can go by the place during the previous day and find someone working to price and prepare the sale. Once in awhile you can talk them into letting you see the stuff and maybe even buy some items before the crowds arrive. Your friends and colleagues will think you have all the luck, and won't understand how you do it!

## Guard Your Pile!

If you go to a sale and find treasures you like, you need to protect your territory and property. More than once, I have been out foraging with my wife and then discovered with a shock that her little pile was violated by another shopper. You need to realize that unless there is a big sold sticker on items, they all look like fair game. Luckily, we have been fortunate to convince the seller these were our selections and turn the sale back in our favor. After all, we saw and grabbed the items first. Once we even paid for an item downstairs, and later found it missing, only to find someone else upstairs paying for it! This can really cause fur to fly!

If you are not careful, it can ruin your day to lose out on an item you had your heart set on. It's just as bad if you cause someone else the same frustration. Always carry the stuff around with you and take it to your car after paying for it. Never leave a pile of stuff alone or it might be grabbed. After all, you saw a bargain, it's likely someone else will also see it as a great deal.

## Estate Sales (Your Own)

If you ever had to dispose of an estate, you know how much work is involved. I did this for my parents' estate, during the writing of this book. I guess it could be considered part of my training and experience, and will help me to explain it to you better by having gone through it myself. This is better than trying to describe it from the sidelines. After reading this, hopefully you will have a better appreciation of what goes on.

After my mother and father passed away, we found that we needed to clean the house out and divide the estate. This was all very interesting for me, because I had attended many similar sales and wondered what the family was going through as they held a sale.

Of course, the first thing is dealing with the emotions and the grief of your loss. The next stage is dealing with the matters at hand, like insurance, and bank accounts and other official matters. The next stage is going through and finding all the memories and treasures. Then we had to decide who got what on these items and the work started.

We sorted and organized. We tossed out lots of absolute garbage. We displayed and arranged throughout the house all of the various items. We did a lot of cleaning.

We decided to sell it ourselves. First of all as families (using a three way split, my two brothers and myself) we went through the house and decided who wanted what. There were items that each of us gave to mom & dad that we automatically received back. We then determined the items that were things our parents wanted us to have individually. And then we discussed our needs (like an appliance) and wants. It was amazing how it all seemed that we got what we wanted and needed with not a lot of negotiating, arguing, or even overlap in desires.

After everything was divided and removed, we sorted, cleaned, and priced much of the stuff. I had a good friend of mine come in and help me price the collectibles. He has much more expertise in certain areas I don't collect, and just charged the estate by the hour. It was very helpful and I'm sure it paid off in the value of what was sold.

We listed an ad in the local daily classifieds, and put up fluorescent signs on all the busy street corners and the front lawn. The morning of the sale we had a huge crowd. Publicity was very successful—security wasn't.

People were jerks. They made a mess as they rummaged through the stuff. They broke stuff, and stole items. They changed price stickers on things. Negotiating is fine, in fact, I encourage it, but the demands some of these people had were absolutely ridiculous.

There was a metal scrap lady who came up to me at the sale. She had a ploy I will warn you about. She came first to me and asked how much for all the metal scrap she could find. I asked her to give me a better description. We went downstairs, and she pointed out old galvanized pipes, and rods and stuff dad had. I just told her to fill up a box and I'd price it. When she returned, her box had a few little pipes and a couple of the pieces she showed me, but in the box were the old turn-of-the-century door lock mechanisms, handles and hardware. There were also chains that were attached to antique glass bowl lamps that were downstairs. Stuff like that. She was picking for an antiques hardware supplier. What a snake!

We made some money. I even brought in some of my own personal stuff to sell, and sold a lot of it. I guess it was a success, but I don't think I'd do it that way again. But the education was valuable to me. I suppose that what we lost in selling too low and from theft or breakage, we made up in some cash, experience, and knowledge. (Oh, and I made some very valuable contacts too.)

The reason I write about this is to help you learn. I always wondered about how these people felt as we looked through their parents and grand-parents belongings. In doing this myself, the main thing I learned was that the people who are buying from you are a solution. You have to get rid of stuff. You can't and don't want to take it all. You have already separated out the memories. Now it's just stuff.

I also learned better and hope to help you have more respect for these people. It's fine to negotiate and it's okay to get good deals. But don't insult these people or yourself with a lack of integrity and don't be dishon-est. Your experience may tell you the price is cheap for something. They might just want to get rid of it any price and be done with it.

How is the best way to do an estate sale?

I think your choices are as follows:

1. Do it yourself. (This is lots of work, no expertise, get all profit, hard to cover all the bases, messy.)

2. Hire it out to an estate company. (They work, they get a hefty percentage, and they take care of it all.)

3. Auctioneer. (They do as above, but may get a lot more, or less in some cases, best security, big percentage, handle each item, best documentation, but they won't do it if the family has picked all of the good items.)

4. Sell a piece at a time to dealers. (Good luck, it would take forever, and gas mileage, time, knowledge...well it wouldn't be good except for just a few items.)

**Tip:** If you sell yourself, keep all the items worth over $10 in the same room as you (the cashier). Put all items that are tiny, and can be hidden in the hand in a small case. Only have one entrance and exit.

I think, in our situation, we should have hired it out to a local estate sale liquidator, yes, it would cost, but I think we would have made it up on the other end by the extra margin they would have made on it.

Now, for you as a picker, what does all of this mean? You now know better what kind of estate sale you're going to; family, professional, etc. You also could, as you gain experience, offer your services either by word of mouth, or by actually starting a company and advertising, etc.

I've also got to say this, if you ever see theft or dishonesty, while at these sales, stop it. Help out the heirs.

Having your own estate sale is a very educational event.

The family is all involved and at least curious, if not anxious, to see how and what is divided. Many times there can be struggles, but fortu-nately, we were all pretty good with each other. Ours was a three-way split.

*"Remember, you have a 50/50 chance at the auction— you either get the item or you don't!"*

We walked through the house, and made our wishes known about what we wanted. There was give and take, and negotiations, and everything worked out well. It was amazing to see how we all really had different wants.

## Auctions

**There are no friends at auctions.**

Auctions are an exciting experience, and I emphasize experience! There's a high level of energy and emotion that accompanies an auction. People want, wish, and hope. Sometimes you can get an unbelievable deal at an auction. Often you can pay extremely high prices if you are not watching or planning. Planning is very important, because most people cannot make good decisions quickly enough while the auctioneer is spouting off. The fervor is what drives the selling of the goods. The same goods can sit for weeks and months in a dealer's shop or booth and never sell at a better price than at some bid prices.

People can't stand the fact that others will get a good deal and they themselves lose out. This pride is the engine that moves the auction along. Watch the auctioneer and learn how he does it. Sometimes he lets things go quite low just to get things going. The auctioneers control the audience.

When you arrive at an auction, you will usually see items sorted into lots. These lots are usually the same types of products. The lots are numbered. You will also see a marvelous assortment of people. Usually an interesting collection in itself. I usually see dealers and pickers recognized at other places. You will see people taking lots of notes, and whispering to each other. Some have cell phones and make calls, I assume to get a sale before the auction starts, but probably more to get permission from someone at home to buy.

After awhile they start taking their place in the chairs. The auctioneer starts with all of the rules and explanations. They might tell you the order the lots will be bid. They might say they can do about 100 to 120 lots per hour.

The auction starts. There are many fast decisions made. Some are good deals, some are not. People are pleased or disappointed. It gets exciting and fun and interesting. After awhile you will notice how the auctioneer and the audience develop and warm up together.

I remember an auction where the auctioneer kept it going between myself and someone in the back of the room. He got me quite high before I finally bought it. I never did turn around to see who I was bidding against. There's a good possibility there really was not a bidder behind me. Nah, that doesn't really happen, does it?

I know that regulars or the old pros at certain government auctions are said to bid newcomers way up, and then let them buy it way too high in order to discourage them from encroaching onto their territory. Often the novice sees their error, and leaves without paying for the stuff, and the old pro has a chance to pick it up on a later bid time or date.

What is loads of fun, is to win a bid for a whole section of product or a "lot" that you did not have a chance to completely inspect. You then get to search through it finding fun treasures and surprises.

As planning was mentioned above, you should always look over the merchandise carefully while the pressure is off. Take good notes. Read over the notes in a quiet time before the auctioning starts. Decide beforehand what you really wish to buy, and how much is the price you would like along with the highest price you would pay. Be sure you have the money! Realize if you bid and win, it's yours.

Try to ignore the excitement. You're simply there for a good deal. If someone else wants to pay a high price, they deserve what they get. What I want is a good deal. The item you might lose, may be a "one-of-a-kind" but there are countless "one-of-a-kinds" out there. Yes, there are good opportunities, but you have to plan, and think quick. Take good notes of the bidding for future reference. There are no friends at auctions. If you want it, get it. No one is nice to the other guy. This business is not for the timid. Remember, you have a 50/50 chance at the auction—you either get the item or you don't!

## Storage Unit Auctions

These can be a lot of fun. It's too bad it's at someone else's expense. You see, when you rent a storage unit, you sign an agreement that says you will let the landlord sell your property in the storage unit if you don't pay your bill.

They advertise and sell the items at whatever someone is willing to bid. Usually a small crowd gathers around and the unit is opened up, you look from the outside, not able to pick through or inspect it. Just look in and make your bid. The winner gets it all and removes it all that day. You get the treasure and the junk. The sale is usually fairly informal, with minimal competition. The items are varied and interesting.

With these and all the other well kept secrets out there, you can really fill up a house fast! So hopefully you have a good outlet to sell the stuff. Otherwise you need a large storage area, or warehouse to store and process and sell from.

## Auctions that are "Too Good to Believe"

I was excited to see in the newspaper a major auction in our local area. The large ad told of an amazing assemblage of collections from millions of dollars in oriental rugs to glassware and antique furniture, to gold, silver, and countless priceless items. It was to be held in a very exclusive home that was also to be auctioned off.

I first wondered who this person could be, that had collected all of these treasures. Then I wondered about the story behind the sale. Were they in trouble financially or with the law? Was it an estate sale of a famous personality? I could hardly wait.

My wife and I went to the auction, and after a quick search, found that this was nothing more than a sales organization with a fantastic, but deceiving, way to confuse the public into paying too much for worthless junk. They had large mahogany antiqued furniture. And yes, there were vases and glassware and rugs and quilts. But it was all decorator items. It was stuff they imported from India and China, and they removed the country of origin labels from the items and auctioned them off. There were large bronzes after Remington which tells me they were counterfeits. What a scam.

This was what is called a salted auction. Any coins and silver and antiques that were there were nothing more than a few goodies they bought at a coin shop or an antique store to make the place look good.

*"When I travel to a show, I spend many weeks in preparation, a lot of which is done with pencil and paper."*

They did the whole thing in cahoots with a local Realtor who found a way to get hundreds of people through the house she had listed.

We found our way downstairs where we peeked into the triple car garage and found where they had hundreds of these cheap antique reproductions they had imported, all wrapped up in bubble pack and stacked to the ceiling. There were dozens of these big bronze reproductions laying all over. I saw one sell to one individual for over $1000. After thinking about it, I wonder if even some of the higher bidders were there to work the innocent (but stupid) bidders to higher levels.

I'm sure that the lucky bidders got their treasures home and found out much too late that they had bought cheaply made, but expensive decorations. By then, the auction company would be long gone, doing it to someone else.

The whole thing made me remember the house parties where cheap imported decorations were sold to housewives in the 70s. After awhile, you would see the same pictures of owls in autumn colors, or sconces with candles in all the homes in the neighborhood.

## It's Show Time!

It is always a very educational and enlarging experience for pickers, collectors, and dealers to attend a major trade show or swap meet. Usually there is a nationally advertised show on just about any specific collectible. Sometimes these shows can be a week long or longer events. They can draw hundreds or even thousands of people. Some shows host auctions, swap meets, symposiums and unbelievable displays.

Some dealers do several of these shows per year, from which they make the bulk of their entire year's income. Some collectors attending the show save their mad money for an entire year just to spend it all at these shows. There are numerous good deals, and there are countless trades. There is stuff available here that you will never see anywhere again.

When I travel to a show, I spend many weeks in preparation, a lot of which is done with pencil and paper. I make a list of all the possible things I want to find or buy. I also list certain supplies I might need to purchase at the show. I keep the list handy because I know I'll get ideas and thoughts to add to it. I also keep a list of all the people I want to see and any questions I need to ask them on information I seek. I have a list too of the things I want to take as trade stock or things I hope to sell. On my list is all of the things I need to take like business cards, cameras, and personal items.

I go trying to learn as much as I can. Because of this, I write down various goals and things to research while at the show. It might be as simple as gathering price information on new items I see or good contacts I seek from the people I meet. I often try to venture out in other areas in the city, seeing museums and other interesting spots while traveling in the vicinity.

I try and read my notes from the previous shows I attended to remind me of events, etc., which can help me at the next show. I keep a journal on such things. This organization always pays off and keeps me successful. Plus it pumps me up before the show! You might also ask friends and customers what items to pick up while at the show. This can help you fund some or all of the traveling expenses!

While at the show, I always pick up as many business cards, price lists, catalogs and show guides I can find. Many times you can find club newsletters which are full of good information. I also write various notes all over the front of the cards I gather, noting prices of things the dealer has, their specialty, etc.

Sometimes people beat themselves up trying to find items first, before anyone else gets a chance to see items at the show. Some dealers actually bring items for their good customers to offer it to them first. This pre-selling of items is good for the dealer, and for the collector. If you are a collector, you may get a call on good stuff if you have it on some dealer's want list. If you placed a wanted ad in a classified ad, they also might have something to sell you at the show if they know you attend.

If your trade show features a swap meet, realize that there is a

"I usually put a little sign out with my cards telling people what I collect. This has been truly amazing! I have had people come in the show, see my sign, ask me to step outside, and show me their stuff before they show it to anyone else."

published start time or day, and there is the real start time or day. Many times there are eager shoppers and buyers that do some (or a lot of) selling before the meet opens. Depending on the show, it may actually be all over before the actual advertised day it starts! I've attended certain shows where dealers start as much as a week before! By the time many show attendees even arrive, there are items that have been sold and marked up several times and traded places on dealers' tables back and forth! The rumors of the killer stuff that was sold early really gets folks excited. Here's that early bird scenario again.

You might have a long list of needs and wants you bring to the show. Always note a price you would be willing to pay before attending. You might be very pleasantly surprised when there to find it at a much lower cost. Besides, it helps you make quicker decisions. Be flexible and satisfied even if you don't fill your want list. You'll probably find a few things but you'll find many more things you didn't know you wanted until you get to the show.

People watching at these shows is a blast! There are the real shysters, whose honesty you question. There are those who look wanton and lust after everything they see, and lots of good regular folks. People are there to make speeches on their specialty.

Go to the conferences. Walk around and learn as much as you can.

Study the displays. Try trading. Involve yourself as much as you can and you'll find these big shows are really worth the effort!

## Shows, Swap Meets, Sales etc.

I always go not knowing what to expect. It's sort of like going to a movie you know nothing about. You are just waiting to be delighted and entertained. I know that as the day unfolds:

1. I'll gain new contacts, whether customers, suppliers, friends, or competition.
2. I'll learn something!
3. I just might sell something!
4. I will hopefully do some good trading.
5. I'll most likely buy something.
6. I will have some new literature to study.
7. I will have a good time.

I usually put a little sign out with my cards telling people what I collect. This has been truly amazing! I have had people come in the show, see my sign, ask me to step outside, and show me their stuff before they show it to anyone else. I literally did the deal inside, and nobody even knew what they missed!

I had someone come up, see the sign, ask me a few questions, go home and get something and sell it to me. Other collectors there never knew what happened. This particular person later invited me to his home where he sold me another fantastic piece. A few weeks later, he called me with even more good deals! I have had two people on two occasions have me follow them out to their car and give me for free, items I advertise that I collect.

Every case listed above describes deals where I was out very little money or no money and involved items selling in the hundreds of dollars in current market value! Really!

I usually go through some of the same routines in preparing for and attending most swap meets. I usually get real excited. The anticipation just about kills me. I know I will have an experience. I make all of my lists of things to look for. I make lists of people to see. I list all of the questions I may have that I want answers for, like pricing, etc. I make lists of the stuff I'll get ready to try and sell and trade away. I also note all the other things I usually prepare to make the sale a success (tape, scissors, etc.).

The day of the swap meet is usually interesting. I go through all sorts of emotional gyrations like, anticipation, excitement, discouragement, envy, happiness, and euphoria. It's fun to meet new contacts. It's a blast to trade for or just buy a fantastic deal. This is why we do it. It's the pleasure and thrill of the hunt. It's the benefit of the profits. And it's the enjoyment of our field of interest.

It's also great to get rid of stuff so you have more room.

# Chapter 5:

# The Well-prepared Picker

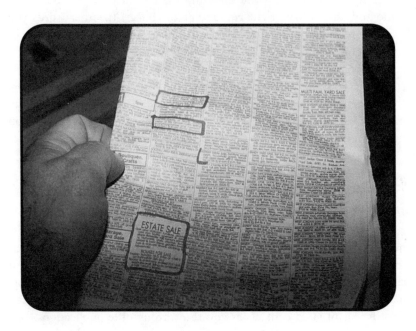

## Lucky Me!

Luck is only one thing; it is essentially chance. If you want luck, you don't want very much. Think of this list of things that might add lots of value to the luck you're hoping for:

Work, effort, hunches, opportunities, preparation, listening, ideas, study, knowledge, creativity, timing, talking, asking, investing, risking, trying, advertising, promptness, moving quickly, wanting, goal setting, skills, tips, secrets, savvy, organization, calling, market knowledge, follow up, follow through.

So if you think someone is lucky, look a bit closer. Simply put:

**"If you have more irons in the fire, you have more hot deals!"**

My father declared once, "I don't see how you "fall into" so many good deals!"

I guess it's like falling into a mine shaft. In order to fall into the mine shaft you have to be near the mine. In order to be near the mine you have to have a map showing you where it is. You might need to have someone take you there. You need the right vehicle to get you to the mine and have all the right equipment to collect. In other words you have to plan to "fall into" the good deals. You have to do lots of prospecting. You need to talk to people. You need to pass out cards and get exposure. You have to follow up on leads and hunches.

When you are out looking for a mine, you find little pieces of ore that sometimes lead you to the vein. The more material you remove and move in the vein, the more ore you get. It's the same kind of clues you need to follow when you are out picking!

## Finding Good Contacts in the Antique Classifieds

There are available, many antiques and collectibles magazines, newsletters, and periodicals. These can be of general interest as well as special interest publications. Some are issues you will wish to keep, and collect all copies for reference. Some have timely and perishable information; others have good material to refer to over the years. You can find dozens of good contacts as you read through the publications. You should try to organize these contacts in a Rolodex file or whatever you are using. This makes it convenient to refer to when you find something you need to sell or talk to an expert, etc. For some of the newspaper type publications, I don't mind cutting the ad right out and taping it to my card. Others, I just copy the name and other needed

Lucky me!

information. Then I organize them by topics, wants, or interests. This could be taken further if you wish and placed on a computer in a searchable database. Then, as you need to find an expert or wish to sell a certain type of collectible or antique, you can find the right contacts.

This helps you when you have an opportunity to buy something but want to presell it. (That is, find a customer before you purchase it or even bid on it.) More often than not, these contacts will give you wonderful information on what to look for, what to watch out for, and even give you ball park appraisals. Your long distance phone call just might result in a good profit, or it could save you from a disaster or help you avoid bad deals. Your contact might be something like this:

"I saw your ad in an edition of.... I recently came across in a thrift store an xyz, model abc. I know you deal in this stuff, and I need your help. I'll probably keep it for myself, but I don't know. They want $XXX for it; is that too much to pay?"

Your responses could be like this:

—"I'm sorry, I do not give appraisals over the phone" (This is probably a poor contact).

—"If you can get it for $100, I'll double your money!" (This could be good for you, but make sure you work out arrangements like freight, payment, etc. up front).

—"No, if you buy it for $100 they're ripping you off, hey, I'll sell them to you for that!" (Good helpful contact, thanks for the help!)

—"Well, you have to be careful, some models have a broken ..., you can tell right off if it's the good one everybody wants, because it has a ... or, only the red ones have any collectible value..." (This is a great contact! This is valuable information you are receiving, it makes you an expert. You should work with this contact in the future and develop a good dealer/picker relationship. Buy stuff from and sell this person stuff!)

—"No, you should call such & such company—they are the experts." (Thank them for their honest help, and find out what they specialize in while you're on the phone, you never know where it will lead!)

If they know they're probably not going to have a chance at buying what you have, or if they're not interested right now, they will probably be pretty honest with the valuation they give. You might hear an answer like, "You paid $5? Yeah, it's a good deal, we sell them all day long for at least $30 each in any condition!"

Here's how you might begin the picker/dealer relationship. Tell them you see this sort of stuff often. Ask what prices they pay pickers for these items. Some might only offer paying you double what you pay, but guarantee to buy all you find. Others will gladly pay you "keystone" or one half, or the going retail price. So search for good dealers who always seem to have the money and are willing to buy what you find.

Keystone—is that fair? I mean really, one half of the retail price? If an item is "worth" a hundred bucks, why don't you hold out for the full bore price? First of all, can you afford to wait for the money? Remember the law of turnover. You make more money on turning your dollars over and keeping cash as a fluid, working power, than by holding on trying to make a bit more profit. This dealer you work with does the same thing. He or she has to turn over the entire inventory a certain amount of times to realize any profit. This extra the dealer makes by selling retail is worth it too, because of the overhead they have that you don't. The dealer might have rent and advertising and utilities and store fixtures that he pays for that you don't have to worry about.

If you buy something for a dollar and sell it for ten times that amount, and then see that the dealer doubles that price, is it fair? You bet it is. As long as he can keep selling these things at this high price, he'll keep buying stuff from you! Your increase was pretty good too, remember? As you get closer to the dealer you also get more information, because they will tell you more about what they want and tips, etc. This is free training. Make sure you write it down and review it.

Make sure of how much material they can use. You might just buy too much and be stuck with inventory. Realize that styles, fads, and tastes all change. Have them tell you what is needed to protect the products, for shipping, storage, etc. Care and cleaning tips are also invaluable.

**Law:** As a dealer finds you are a good source, they are also, in turn, a better source for their customer!

## Want List or "It's In My Little Black Book"

Within your card index, you should have a specific "want list." This goes a bit beyond the list of contacts by topic or experts. This comes from the various dealers, collectors, and others you find advertised or even spoken wants you hear. You can start with the specialties you are particularly interested in and later add all different types of subjects. You might be interested in furniture. You could list others who buy furniture and sort it by series or period. As mentioned, you could then add those looking for furniture, hardware, or books, etc.

As you go along, add art, toys, or other book topics. After all, you will be out and about, and find all kinds of things while you are looking for your items. This way you will have a resource list, and a potential customer file. You can then "pick" for these other folks, and make extra funds to pursue your own specialty!

This can be a very interesting and powerful tool. You can be as elaborate as you wish, entering all the contacts into a computer database, or you could be as simple as having a card file or Rolodex file.

One simple method is to take some 3x5 cards and place them in a standard format as shown in the example:

---

# WANT: Glassware, Roseville

### Collects all types, has large collection. Will buy chipped pieces. Sells in the Raccoon Den

### Antique Mall on Hill Street.
Pays about 1/2 of list. (More for rare pieces)

## Joey Hansen
XXX-XXXX

---

This can be simple or detailed as needed. Put "want" in the upper corner, and file by the listed topic. There is also plenty of room on the back of the card to take a few "live" notes as you contact or hear good information about the contact. You will build a very important and valuable file of information by doing this. This will be a strong edge to keep you ahead of the competition.


## Tickler File

This is a separate file you keep for all of those leads you find or people give you to "check out one of these days." You should follow up on some as soon as you can, where others could possibly wait. Every time you have a good idea, inspiration, or overhear some great tip, put it here. You may find lots of excellent leads as you get into this business, but unless you keep track of them, they are lost. You need to develop a "tickler file." Do you want to be the one to close the big deals? If you want to be successful buying and selling estates and collections, or even just pick and sell,you need to check back regularly and have lots of deals cooking. Literally, some deals can take years to complete! Estates may lie dormant, people stay undecided, change their minds, or may not be ready to sell various property.

You might be fortunate and have a friend who is watching out for you and gives you a good lead. Or you might just be lucky and fall into information of some items you like for sale. Better yet, you may be advertising for these items and someone answers the ad. Sometimes it's a garage, a basement, a storage unit, or an entire house of stuff you are anxiously looking for. It might be just one item that is valuable and unique.

You contact the owner or the heir and it might just come together. Because it sounds so positive and hopeful, you still need to check back; someone else could easily "scoop" you—even if it looks as if there is no competition!

## You Need to Check Back

Often people forget, or lose your name and number, or can't recall the details of the deal (money, list of items you want, etc.). What's really discouraging is to find out someone else firmed up the deal while you put off calling.

If you can, leave a printed business card with your interests and date written on it. This will be a reminder to your "client." Next write it in your tickler file. The tickler file you use could be a list or cards or even a calendar or day planner.

You'll be absolutely amazed how many deals you'll get before the competition even knows there was one. Your colleagues and buddies will be dumbfounded about how you seem to be the best picker in your field!

## Glue, Polish, and Spit

You can learn how to fix and clean stuff, but if you really want to gain a skill don't just repair, but actually restore if possible. Collectors and dealers never like to see any kind of obvious modifications, but a true restoration adds so much more value to an item. If it is a very valuable piece, make sure you know what you are doing, or leave it to a qualified person to do. Most serious collectors want to do their own restorations, so be very careful.

Many pickers, understanding the importance of quality restorations,

Will you tell me your secret?

won't do much more than light cleaning, or gluing of broken pieces, but then sell it to waiting dealers who specialize in restoring . It is good to know what kind of cleaners will work on various products you handle, for example, those items made of plastic or items painted long ago. Decals and intricate paint should not be touched if at all possible. One absolutely horrible thing that even some experienced antique dealers do is to brush rusted metal with a wire wheel, that leaves a very distinctive texture on the metal. Then they simply paint it black. It kind of ruins the piece.

Some wonderful books (see the reading list) on refinishing are available if you really want to study the correct way. Have a real good talk with each of your dealer friends and possible customers, asking what you should or shouldn't do. Find out in what kind of condition they prefer you to bring it to them.

## So Will You Tell Me Your Secret?... Well, OK!

People like to boast and brag. It's very interesting what pride does to people. You might want to try a little research like I did to write this book and see what I mean.

Pretend that you are a reporter gathering information for a research project. Talk to people and ask them questions. You will be flabbergasted to see how much they will tell. They may be keeping back secrets consciously in a way, but be telling you exactly what you want in a different way. For example, they may keep secret the location they found an important item, but then tell you of how they negotiated for the item. Or, they will tell you flat out how they went about finding the source for something good, a way you never considered before, giving you what should have been the most protected information and secrets. They often will give you valuable pricing tips. They may tell you what styles are most popular, etc.

If you are specializing in one area, and they know it, but you ask about one of their other interests, they really open up. After all, they don't feel you're a competitor as much. But you are learning. Ask questions like, "So who buys all that glassware you find" they will probably tell you right off (write it in your card file). Another question might be, "So, who is the best person to talk to about this style of furniture?" Pickers all know each other. Break into the business by asking questions. You'll find it's a small world.

Develop an eye for the good stuff!

## How to Develop an Eye for the Good Stuff

When you are out and about picking, you are constantly learning. Every day is different. I suppose that's why people stick with this. There are so many different and interesting things!

When you're looking for things, you may find items you may have seen before, or something completely new to you. This new item may show you evidence to believe it is very old, or rare, or expensive. So what do you do?

1. You might plunk down the cash and take it.
2. If you can, get the seller to hold it for 24 hours (but they have to keep it out of sight from other potential buyers!)
3. If you really like it, want it, have the room for it and can afford it, by all means purchase it. You should have it. This is a good measure of how much you like it. If you get stuck with it, you won't mind at all—just get it.
4. If you can make a phone call to an expert or especially a potential buyer, do so. (but please remember caller ID!) I actually did that, I called a collector from another collector's house about an item. They were not aware of each other before that time.
5. If it is cheap and you can afford to lose the investment, just buy the thing.
6. If you do walk away from it, at the very least, try and find out about the thing later, now that you have had the experience. Go look it up in a price guide, talk to an expert, or check out a dealer who may have some. You will know for next time. Who knows, if it is a good piece, you may discover later on that it could very well still be there. It's happened.

This is all part of the learning. This is your "college of picking knowledge." You buy books, read, and study. You pay tuition by buying and investing, and you have tests (by winning some and losing some).

## Abracadabra... Poof! ... It's Now Worth Fifty Bucks!

So, you're getting good at spotting good stuff. You see it and swoop it up, but something really bugs you. How in the world do I price it?

Some people who specialize in certain areas have an exceptional eye for varied merchandise. They may even publish an interesting list or catalog. You also see other individuals who grab for the weirdest stuff.

You cannot believe they pass up your treasures and go for junk and are absolutely tickled to get it.

Both of these folks are making money. Both of them can spot a good deal. They may have clientele that wants these items. But how do they know how much to sell the stuff for? How much profit do they make? Why or how can anything have a price measure attached to it?

It comes down to experience, knowledge of the products, the market, and hard work. Oh yes, and good notes. Sure, price guides may give some help or at least comparative relation to some sort of rarity valuation. But actual study of ads, lists, and catalogs is the best measure.

Keep track of prices on stuff you have an interest in or may have exposure to. Compare prices at stores, talk to collectors, save ads, and write down model numbers and prices. You are on your way to becoming an expert.

After awhile, this knowledge will go with you as you're out picking. The stuff you find will be like cash in your hands. Good deals will be known. You'll be a better trader, and dealer.

Constantly read books, catalogs and magazines. Be open to new areas of interest, expanding your picking field. Get interested in the history of the stuff. Compare and write down notes! Go to shows and meets. Update often because trends and interests and values change. Be careful to inspect condition. The best stuff, or mint-in-box items, are of course priced much higher.

## There is Power in Praise

Thank you notes can be very valuable tools. True friendship is also a wonderful side benefit. You get good ins or contacts, reliable suppliers, and have more loyal customers.

So be honest and helpful when you can. Always give a bit more than the customer expected. Do favors and ask for favors—it breaks the ice. Use a person's name often and remember birthdays and anniversaries. When you see a good reason, send a note. It all comes back to you. It makes this business much more pleasurable.

## Become an Expert!

To be a professional when it comes to picking, you have to be an expert in one or more of the fields on the items you pursue. You might already be an expert in various subjects because of a job or training.

Become an expert!

You may have a strong interest in something you've casually read or just thought about, that now you really want to study. You might have a talent in an area that has a valuable history, and has items related that you want to find. You also may have collected some things as a child that you are ready to brush the dust off of in the attic. Some people may have a geographical advantage, living in an area that has a lot of interesting and important memorabilia or artifacts that can still be found, or have historical industry products that were produced locally in the past.

Become an expert! Find out what your hot button is and then find out everything you possibly can about it. Go to the library, visit museums, manufacturers, distributors, local or nearby shows, and special meets. Frequent dealers and stores dealing in the items. See if there is a club or association in your area, and get involved. Talk to old timers in the field, they have wonderful knowledge. Subscribe to newsletters and magazines and buy collector's guides to your products. Search the Internet; you'll get unbelievable amounts of information, ideas, and leads!

As you immerse yourself, study, get excited, try and fail, try and succeed—you'll be an expert in a relatively quick time.

## Book Learning

"A little bit of knowledge is a dangerous thing."

"Jack of all trades, but expert of none?"

Start a library! Read!

Find out about all sorts of stuff. After all, stuff is what you are out looking for. I send for catalogs from both home and work. I thumb through as many as I can. I look at things: machinery, hardware, tools, and what-cha-ma-call-its. I see how they are shaped and built and try to figure out what they do. I've always been interested in equipment, tools, and industries. Who knows, it may have started when I was in elementary school and went to various manufacturers and companies on our field trips. I've always liked to either take apart stuff, or fix broken things.

I scan the books and catalogs so I can learn how and with what things are done. As a result, I have profited well when out picking. I also find I am more of an expert in my work and to others, because of my knowledge of things. It's interesting, pays off, and I profit in all kinds of ways.

So now when I'm out at a swap meet or other likely spot, and find a gadget or thingamajig and it's a dollar or two, I pick it up. I know who uses these, and I bet I can sell it. I've bought an expensive piece of test equipment for just $25 and sold it a week later for $1200!

Book learning.

Get familiar with brand names. Find out which are the most expensive and why. Ask around. "I see some of the same names show up all the time when I'm out picking, what should I be watching for?" People will tell you. They want you to know because there is a better possibility to buy something you find for a good deal!

All of this works for antiques, collectibles, industrial equipment, and just about anything.

You might even get a file cabinet (when you're out picking, of course!) and start a literature file of catalogs that interest you for reference. This is good to have for pricing guides too.

As you study and immerse yourself in the subject, you'll add knowledge, gain appreciation, and become an expert very quickly. You will also see how various industries and products were connected. This helps you identify items you come across. Even just looking at pictures will help you.

Try and visit various libraries in your area. University and other major libraries are especially helpful. These institutions carry many rare and out-of-print books and publications you'll never see otherwise. Some even sell or trade their old and duplicate books!

Research at the library should include magazines and industrial publications too. You'll find contacts for suppliers, dealers, and distributors in your field. See what your local library has in antique and collectibles resource guides. Usually you will find shelves full of current books. You will also be fortunate if you find older out-of-print guides and information which is valuable when researching certain finds.

As you also study, find the Thomas Register (a thirty volume catalog of just about everything, approximately 8-10 feet long!) at the library. You will see the value of this and other references when pricing, buying, or selling stuff you're finding. You can then find many contacts (especially with toll free numbers) to use when reference is needed. Put these names in your contact directory. You can call companies listed in the Thomas Register and ask who are local dealers and distributors for stuff you find locally. You can also ask for current prices on items still made. Some of these listed companies buy back products, refurbish, and re-market them. They could refer you to the local distributor or dealer to buy your items.

If you find a box of widgets, call around to find the regular selling price and then offer them for one half or one third to the dealer. They may buy them all, giving you a healthy profit! I have been involved in these types of deals often. Many folks do this and make a good living.

You can also find sources for parts, manuals and literature, etc. You will then find (as you are out and come across items) you have more contacts to help you sell to or just get pricing information, so you can sell locally.

The more you read, the more reference material you have, the more study you do, the more success you'll have. You'll be further ahead of your competition, enjoy it more, and find much better products! There is probably a correlation between the dollars you make and the time you study. I wish I could tell you how many dollars an hour you increase for every hour you read!

## Literature, Paper, etc.

Realize that books, magazines, ads, manuals, and paper on collectibles are also collectible. So find out more before you cut up old out-dated information.

New collectors coming into the field love to get a hold of out-of-print magazines and journals on the items they collect. Some even place ads for old issues wanted in order to put together a set, etc.

You should begin buying and picking for books in your specialty or various specialties. Never pass up any books on various antiques or collectibles. These will be a valuable reference. Besides, picking for books is lucrative. You'll always be able to sell them if you find they are of no use to you. Other valuable references are the historical catalogs and books on the history of your field. Vintage catalogs from manufacturers and distributors have loads of wonderful information. You can find model numbers, photos, original prices, parts and accessories, etc. These old catalogs are very valuable and sought by collectors. You can sell them easily. Also look for the histories of industries, companies, and biographies of those individuals important to your particular specialty.

## Dear Diary

Keep a journal or diary of what you do. This is very valuable information you are writing. As you make a deal, you just may need to find the person's name and phone number again. For example, you might go by a home and buy something they had for sale. Later, even months later you learn about something someone you know is looking for. You remember seeing one at this guy's house! You go to your notes, find the phone number, call and ask about the item, and you may have made another good deal.

Always keep nearby in the journal another page that has your hot list. This hot list, similar to your tickler file, is a very, very valuable part of your success.

Everyone has deals that never quite happened. Maybe the person has something buried away in the garage to show you one day, or has an item he wants to sell, but it's in the very back of the storage unit. This page is no more than a person's name and phone number and a sentence or word of what they might have. Some of these deals take months or even years to complete; some never materialize. But, some are golden!

When you have a minute, read through the list. If you haven't heard the status lately, call and see what's going on. Ask if they ever found the stuff. Check back, mark your calendar if necessary. This separates you from the wannabees. You will make the best deals. Everyone will wonder how you do it.

## Applied Research

The research associated with this profession is interesting, fun, and exciting.

My wife and I love to frequent antique stores. She goes because of her own enjoyment; I go as part of my research. Yes, it's research in my field. I learn about new, hot collectibles and I study prices. I gain new contacts and customers, that is the antique dealers, themselves. I obtain and leave business cards. We have fun together and both learn an awful lot every time we go out.

Other areas of research can be done in the library. Usually libraries have one or more areas regarding antiques, collectibles, and other types of books in your particular area of study. The same goes for used book-stores. You not only look for books, but you see the value of some of the books you find.

Joining a club can be a marvelous way to research. Usually the information found and disseminated in a club setting is not found anywhere else. It's probably because so many experts are there in the same place. Other collectors can be very valuable to your research. Visit their collec-tions and ask questions—build a relationship. You'll probably end up selling and buying from many of them.

Visit local museums, and also every museum you can visit while trav-eling. Ask questions and learn. Find out what they buy and from whom. Ask if they make exchanges.

Magazines are extremely important. As you read all the new articles and ads, you gain a tremendous amount of knowledge you can't possibly obtain any other way. You literally keep up with what is happening in the market.

There may even be a helpful directory of contacts and suppliers that is unique to your field. Go to every show and specialized swap meet you can, even if it means traveling. Read classified ads and visit auctions.

As mentioned, the Internet and the world wide web are absolutely exploding with valuable information. There is a mail list and a usenet group for the area too. Note, I didn't say there "probably is", I said there is. Check it out.

## Be Selective!

When I first started in the collecting hobby I felt I was way too late. I saw or read about huge collections. I would study magazines and catalogs from dealers who had unbelievable stuff and lots of items. I even remember having a conversation with a nationally known dealer of certain antiques, and telling him I felt like a late comer. I said it looks like all the good stuff is gone! He was very surprised at my statement. I was surprised that he was surprised! He assured me that it was just starting. He said more and more good stuff is coming out now more than ever before. He said he was thrilled and excited about what has been coming available on the market lately.

Be careful! There is a big temptation, especially when you are new, to buy everything in sight related to your new found field of interest. If you don't specialize, you'll end up with lots of junk, less room, less cash, and bewilderment! Remember, there are many good deals out there, more than you can imagine!

You need to continually upgrade and trade off. Turn your treasures over. I say treasures because there is the tendency to consider many old items as irreplaceable.

The tendency is to hoard everything. Some gather the good, complete, valuable products, as well as the broken down, damaged junkers.

You might need a few replacement parts. It may be wise to hang onto certain parts sets to cannibalize and repair the better one that comes along.

When you get larger amounts and wonder what to do, you will want to specialize. You'll want only a certain brand, style, or certain date. Another great idea is to set certain value limits for example: "I won't collect or deal in anything less than $100 in book value. You then sell off, trade off, or dump the lesser stuff as you can. You'll be surprised at what your collection or inventory will look like!

*"Remember, your competition doesn't necessarily have to be another picker or dealer that is after the stuff you want; it might just be lots of regular people that take a fancy to something you're searching for, and buy it on an impulse."*

## Aesthetics

Besides rarity and quality, aesthetics is the highest reason for increased value in a collectible. Understanding aesthetics is both innate and learned. You have in you a certain like and dislike for the looks of things. Those who have a real gift also do well in home decoration and display. You either have an eye for it or you don't. Now don't despair. Some of it can be learned. If you are picking for certain items, you can always memorize all the types of the hot pieces that are popular. A bit of caution: You may have the eye for it, but really want the thing—then it's going to be difficult to sell it. Or you don't have the eye for it and sell important and valuable items much too easily.

Find out what stuff sells for and who wants it. Especially go for the things you want. Find out why everybody wants it. Besides aesthetics, look for:

    historical importance
    rarity or limited production
    beauty   finest quality
    resale value
    certain color or certain series
    fads and trends fame (For example, it may be hot now because
    it was just featured in a magazine)

If you have ever seen a Christies auction catalog it's interesting how they add value to the products that will be auctioned, by listing "Important" in the title. For example they could just say "Antique Toys" and you think one thing, but when they say "Important Antique Toys", it seems to infer lots of other possibilities, such as "could this be the first ones like it ever made," or maybe these were owned by famous children and they have the documents to prove it. They might have been used in a movie as props. Whatever the case, important they are, and they will sell for a bundle.

Part of the determination are the things you look for to judge its condition. Is the case cracked? Is it in the original package? Are all of the original papers with it? Do you have any letters to and from the factory proving ownership and history? Is the finish original or repainted? We've all heard the stories, like the extremely valuable furniture piece that lost most of its value. The owner didn't like the original finish, so he or she stripped and re-finished the entire piece. I have heard of items worth an original $100,000 being worth only $10,000, because of a botch job like this.

You have to know if it is ethical or moral to restore the item, or whether to leave it alone. (When in doubt, by all means leave it alone!) Are replacement or reproduction parts available for the unit? Could they have been used on this one? Is the serial number significant?

## Buried Pyramid

You will notice an interesting phenomenon as you begin to study any particular field. I call it the buried pyramid. I don't recall where I first learned this theory, but I see it in my life often.

As you start with a newfound interest—let's say it's antique furniture, you may have seen something you like and because you know a little about it, have set some goals to find a piece or two. Maybe you start reading up on the subject. This is the tip of the pyramid, sticking out of the sand. It is a small but interesting curiosity. (Note too, this is well-worn by many, and is usually where most people stop.)

As you dig deeper, you gain new fresh understanding. You see how the field widens. You see how much more you didn't know. You discover your pyramid is larger than you imagined! Curiosity turns to fascination. Fascination turns to obsession for some as they try to find the end of it. It's amazing!

You buy more, you trade, you sell. That neat stuff you had to have at first, is of little interest now. Your eyes are opened! The field is immense. You finally admit the only way to comprehend much more is to specialize.

The pyramid exists in all fields. It could be furniture, clocks, glassware, or toys. You'll find more documentation, like books and magazines and literature. You'll discover more people, collectors, and contacts. You'll find dealers, stores, shops, and museums, and be astounded at your discoveries.

## Decisions, Decisions!

We've all seen the sign hanging in an antique store, "The best time to buy an antique is when you see it!"

I really believe this is also the case in picking for items. I can't tell you how many times I have actually left an antique or collectible or junk item at a very good price, deciding to decide later, and upon return find it gone. Yes, there have been times when it's still there, but it's been rare.

So know your stuff, get familiar with prices and strike when the iron is hot. Opportunities do evaporate as quick as they appear.

## Keep Moving!

As I learned years ago in a statistics class, if you ever get lost, your chances of getting found by staying still are far less than by moving around. Your moving around and your rescuers moving around increases the chances dramatically. If you ask, try to check out new places, and follow hunches you'll find more stuff. The person who stays at home waiting for a good deal to come to him doesn't stand a chance. You always get more luck by working hard, and by checking out more leads and places.

## Snap Shots

I call it taking snap shots. It's when you go out picking and take your chances according to your timing. Most pickers move around. You try lots of different places—ones you either just want to check out or places where you've had success in the past. You never know what is going to be put out for sale. You never know where your competition is. Remember, your competition doesn't necessarily have to be another picker or dealer that is after the stuff you want; it might just be lots of regular people that take a fancy to something you're searching for, and buy it on an impulse.

Buried pyramid.

This business is very cyclical. It's wonderful one day or one place, and will change to nothing somewhere else or at a different time. People dispose of items randomly. Don't get discouraged if you don't find anything one day. Just by checking, you'll be that much closer to the next find.

As mentioned before, statistically you could prove it: the more you keep moving, the better your chances are of finding something. Besides, if you don't find anything, that means you still have your money! I've noticed something very revealing. I found myself several times buying an item at a thrift shop that I know just came out of the back room. I picked it up, paid for it, carried it out to the car, and most of the people that ever came into the store that day never saw the item. This happens many times a day. You'll look around and see a bunch of the same old stuff but realize you didn't see the best of it—it's gone.

But then you, on your next trip, will find the prize and they will never see it. That is why I call it a snap shot. An actual photographic snap shot is a very brief period of time that is recorded. Just like in a real photograph, you don't get the whole story. As you pick, you don't know what you'll miss, or will miss out on. I think you get the picture!

## Parlaying

This basically means to take something, and make it worth more. Say I take a dollar out of my pocket, buy something, and sell it for $5. I then take the five dollar bill and buy an item with it, which I in turn sell for twenty dollars. I am parlaying, or building upon my original investment of one dollar. I keep adding my original and subsequent profits—in effect betting the winnings.

There is high risk in doing this, but there are also large rewards. You might discover that the sell time increases with the higher valued items. You will also learn quickly how quality fits into the equation.

I have heard of similar stories, but instead of parlaying to different items, you track the same item through different dealers. I heard a lady at an antique show say some dealers were selling some highly valued collectible from collector and dealer to collector, etc. for the entire week. It ended up selling in the end for a hundred dollars less than it started out! So who knows.

All I know is, when you do parlay yourself, it's a blast to see how your investment can grow in a short time. Keep cool, learn, and have fun.

# Silent Bids: Low Balling

You may have an opportunity to be involved in certain silent bids. Occasionally, some thrift stores have an area where some of their better donations and antiques are displayed and left for bidders to determine the selling price. After a week or so, the bids are reviewed and the winning bidder is notified they can come buy their item. Sometimes you can get a pretty good deal, especially if your item hasn't had any other bidders. But, how do you know? You can't. You have to guess. Is the item you're after something that many people seek? Is the store in a mainstream high traffic area where many collectors have a chance to visit? Historically, have you lost bids to similar items in that store?

Sometimes there are also some real bad shoppers who either don't know their products or just like to pay too much, and their bid causes them to over pay. You might try and do some low balling. Low balling is to bid much lower than the market price. Yes, your chances are less than ever to win the bid, but your chance to win a better profit is much greater. If there are many different items you bid on in a given time, you do have a good chance in getting something, even with low-ball bids.

This is difficult if you really hope you will have the winning bid. But, you may be willing to do so to get a good price.

Let's just say you see an antique in the store that has a restored value of $1,000. This value increases when you clean it up, repair and restore it. It's value as found is $400. That is, if you get it, you know a dealer or collector might pay you $400. You could easily bid $200 or even $250 for the item and feel pretty good about it, right? Or, you could low-ball the bid and hope to get it for $100 or $150. Oh, but you might not get it, right?

I like to chart things out, let's see how we would feel at certain prices on our $400/$1000 item:

If you pay $250 it's OK.
If you pay $200 it's better.
If you pay $175 it's really good.
If you pay $150 it's great!
If you pay $100 it's fantastic!
If you pay $50 it's a steal!
If you pay $10 it's unbelievable and embarrassing.

What you are doing is buying a deal. You have to decide just what deal you wish to purchase. If you think about this chart before you make the bid, you end up with one of these deals if you have the winning bid.

If you have found a way to remove emotion from the bidding, all the better. Sometimes we just really need to have something and bid too high, get stuck with it, tired of it, and have a hard time moving the item. This just frustrates us and ties up our dollars and we essentially bought that kind of a deal.

Sometimes a little studying before the bid, and taking the time to write down pro and con statements before we put down a price will help.

Ask some questions like:

How bad do I really want it? (add or subtract $)

Is it for my own personal collection? (add $)

Is it for resale for a profit? (subtract $)

Is it pre-sold? Do I have a buyer now with cash in hand? (add $)

Do I have the spare cash to buy this right now? (Remember, if you don't get it, you still have your money! You can always find a truly good deal at another time.) Also, make a list of the competitors that are likely to bid on it. Here's the final breakdown:

Value at list price $1,000.

Street price is $800.

As found price is $400.

Highest I'd go is $250.

At $100 I'm sure to lose it.

The ideal price would be $150.

I'm going to bid $180 and I'd feel pretty good about the deal. Then live with the outcome. On small items, like $5-$10 don't sweat it, just go by your gut feeling, and try to pick up a good deal, by low-balling.

## The First & the Last

The assumption is that if you are the first person to a sale, you'll do very well. If you can even be one of the lucky few that are invited to preview a sale before the public is invited, even better. Yes, you'll have the best selection. Yes, you'll have less competition. Yes, you'll have the best finds, deals, sleepers, etc.

The last person to a sale has benefits too!

Here's where you get the best price. Now they just want to get rid of it! You also may get lucky and be there when they happen to find something tucked away and forgot to put on the sale. You can get lot prices on the leftovers. You might even get piles of stuff for free just for hauling it off. Stuff that was priced way too high (and the seller wasn't going to budge on the price) might go dirt cheap at the end of the day. But then again, it might not be there. So don't plan on it, just recognize those end-of-the-day deals and finds when you see them!

## *Tools of the Trade*

It might be good to have a few tools available when you are out in the field picking. These could be kept in your car as a few things you might always want to have with you. A good pocket knife is wonderful. One with a little but sturdy screwdriver is best, especially if the screwdriver blade is good for Phillips and flat blade screws. My little Swiss one is nice. You might go a bit further and get one of those multi-tools that has everything from pliers to knives to bits coming out of everywhere.

Cash, a checkbook, and coins for the phone (unless you use a cell phone) are a must. A tiny magnet might prove useful someday. Flashlights are great, especially in a dark old place that has had old things hidden for years. It's good to have one for looking into old equipment too. You also might want to have a magnifying lens.

Boxes and bags in the car might be handy. And a blanket to cover your car upholstery is very needed sometimes. Here's a good reason for those little wash towelettes in the glove box—old stuff is dirty.

Your little black book with all of the handy numbers of dealers and buyers is invaluable. If you keep a want list, you might want this information available. Be prepared, scouters

# Chapter 6:

# How to Do it Better Than the Other Guy

## Better? How?

By now, you have tried a few of the ideas and techniques discussed while you've been picking for stuff. You also have many of your own secrets that have proven helpful. You have made money and found all kinds of prizes and treasures. The problem is still the other guy.

You have met all kinds. I know, I've seen them too: pickers, dealers, charlatans, and all sorts of wheeler-dealers. Some are clever, some are smart. There are both the successful ones and the ones that don't get it. You'll find the ones you can trust and some that are out-and-out crooks.

Now what?

The first hint is: LEARN. Watch, listen, and find out how and why people do things. You'll come out on top.

I love to play a practical joke once in awhile. I have always told everyone who tries to pay me back that it doesn't matter what they try, I will always be the victor. The reason I can say this, is I hold a secret weapon. This secret is that I always win because whatever they do to me, I can use that idea to get someone else. Ultimately I come out on top. What's really been strange is, most people give up and never pay me back—just by my making the statement of preconceived victory!

As you learn how a colleague picker scooped you on a deal, you get better. No, you didn't get the items, nor did you make the profit, but now you are armed with a bit more knowledge and experience. This also goes especially for bad deals that others make. You learn without losing money!

This chapter is loaded with some good how-to information.

## Why do Some do Better Than Others?

Q: Why is someone successful?
A: Because they grow.

Q: Why do they grow?
A: Because they get involved.

Q: Why are they so involved?
A: Because they have passion.

Q: Why do they have so much passion?
A:: Because they caught the vision.

**Q:** Why do they catch the vision?
**A:** Because they are motivated to.

**Q:** Why are they so motivated?
**A:** Because they have a desire.

**Q:** Why do they have this desire?
**A:** Because they believe.

**Q:** Why is it they believe?
**A:** Because they have an interest.

**Q:** Why do they have an interest?
**A:** Because they are curious.

**Q:** Why are they so curious?
**A:** Because they have questions.

**Q:** Why do they have questions?
**A:** Because they are unsatisfied and they know that there is more!

## Set Good Goals and Never Ever Quit

Goal-setting works in this world as well as any other line of work or venture. As you study and gain likes, tastes, and wants, don't be afraid to set some goals. You may want to find the best or the finest doohickey ever made. You might never find it, but in the looking for it, may find something almost as neat or even much better.

Get a good book (actually find a good book when you're out picking) on goal-setting. Read it, and believe in the ways it tells you to set and accomplish goals. You'll be better for it.

Realize this: you really can have absolutely anything you really want. Just make sure you have good wants.

## Dealers With a Storefront

Those who have a storefront always have an advantage over others, as there are constantly people bringing items to them. This is a form of advertising. People see your place; they might have something like they saw in your display and either bring something similar in to unload or spread the word to others that have things to sell. It brings a lot of stuff on the market that would never have surfaced normally. This is in addition to pickers who bring these dealers many items.

## Free is Good!

After you get involved in a specialty, you might find that occasionally people you know or meet give you stuff...for free! You might have relatives or neighbors call you and tell you to come over, they have something for you.

I know a collector who was fortunate enough to get his antique television collection featured on a television program a few years back. He had many people call asking him to just come on over and pick up vintage televisions from their garages and basements.

One time I received a call from someone that picked up one of my cards at a show. He said I should drive over one day because he had some stuff similar to what I was collecting and selling. He filled up my trunk with books and classic collectible items! Here's a good reason to list all of your interests on your business cards. You'll never know where that card may end up, or when.

You might not be able to get free exposure on television, but what might happen if you approach your local library and ask if you can put a display out on the items you collect? I'm sure you'll have people coming from all directions. Many libraries have beautiful locked display cases set up for purposes just like this.

## Creating Your Own Market Demand

The best way to get the market going on your items is to start or join in on the hype. By hype, I mean the speeches at symposiums, the articles written in newsletters, the talks and show and tell at club meetings, etc. Hype might sound negative, but what I describe here is nothing more than building knowledge which begets interest and appreciation. This then, creates value which makes demand and creates sales. As others learn of the finer points of something antique, they really start to bond with it.

As you see the professionals, what do they do? Christies and Sotheby's publish some of the most magnificent catalogs with absolutely gorgeous full color photography. They write wonderful articles on the history and importance of the products they will be selling. The catalogs are instructive; they tell you why you need to have an item by creating interest.

You might look at some ways to start some action in your particular field of interest in your local area. It will pay off. You will create new collectors. You'll see new stuff comes from all sorts of new sources you didn't even know about. You can find treasures in trash, or with hype you can create new treasures from trash.

Some collectibles, especially those newly emerging or pre-collectible items, need lots of hype to gather and sustain the interest. Those pushing these newer products deemed collectible, use much publicity and advertising to keep interest going.

For you to promote and generate lots of interest, you need to collect the items. You then need to inspire others to collect them. You need to point out your likes and descriptions and define classic features. You need to encourage people who collect stuff like you find because it gets people to establish new wants and it increases values and gives prices meaning.

Sometime, just watch how a good dealer who runs an antique mall works. If some customer asks questions or makes conversation on a particular item in the store he sells it based upon his own affection for it and interest in the item. He hypes it up! The enthusiasm is infectious, and the customer goes home excited about his purchase. Some phrases include:

"Don't you just love those..."

"I really hate to sell that one because..."

"You know, when I saw that come in the store, I..."

"Those are so neat! This one is my favorite, you know why?
(the color, the date, etc.)"

"We sell those as soon as they come in"

"I've had more interest in that lately!"

"I could sell those by the thousands if I could only get that many..."

"These have really taken off lately... (shows an article, etc.)"

These comments give a justification for their passion and it helps them feel better about their expenditure.

Hype is actually a form of advertising. It fans the fire, it plays with pride and for a moment, magnifies their obsession. After all, the process of obtaining an item is always much more pleasurable than actually having it. When you sell an item, or even hint there is competition, it can raise the fervor as several collectors will fight for the same item.

Other ways to accomplish the hype or excitement might include:

1. Start a club with meetings and a newsletter, etc.
2. Have a special showing, inviting certain collectors.
3. Advertise a special swap meet.
4. Have an auction.
5. Publish a newsletter.
6. Become an authority by writing a new book on your emerging collectible.
7. Do a public interest TV spot or local newspaper article on your specialty. The more obscure or esoteric it is, the better chance you'll get a reporter's attention.
8. Place an intriguing ad in the classified that will bring other collectors to you for you to sell to or buy from.
9. Inspire your friends to get into the field.
10. Partner with someone with similar interests.
11. Corner the market on something you feel will be hot. (Be careful!)
12. Put a display in a mall or public library.
13. Rent part of your collection as a display, or mini museum somewhere.
14. Have a special display of items for sale in an antique showcase mall.
15. The Internet. Search for others with the same new interest.

## A Unique Way to Find Stuff

I spoke to a collector who found a great way to find items. He collects a unique, expensive item that is usually hard to find. One night he told me how he did this. It was one of his secrets, but he did not tell me it was a secret, so I share it here. I purposely refrain from telling you what it is, because I don't want to limit your thinking or focus. I really believe this will work with all sorts of items you might be interested in.

Steve would get in his car while on vacation and actually target certain rural areas in his state or others nearby. He would find small town libraries, grocery stores, gas stations, and Laundromats—any place that might have a bulletin board. He'd tack up either a business card or a small poster that said what he wanted. His little signs were very successful. He was finding his treasures in all kinds of strange places. He would then drive to farms and go to barns, garages, and old closed buildings. He'd obtain some very remarkable deals in all kinds of unique places.

## Hang out Your Shingle!

Advertising pays!

You might not have a storefront to hang a sign outside. But you can do other things to announce you are in business. First of all, make up an attention-getting business card. Tell what kind of stuff you pick for. Have them printed professionally. The finer your card looks and feels, the more respect it brings.

---

Always looking for: Old Furniture
Old Watches, Old Fountain Pens, Old Jewelry.

## "GARAGE SALE NUT!"

### Abe Lincoln
Phone 111-111-1111
email xxx@xxx.com

Buy & Sell                                    Trade & Swap

---

Hand out the cards. Leave them at all the sales you visit. (You will get calls and referrals.) If you sell at a show or swap meet put a stack out for people to pick up. Give to friends, collectors, dealers and antique stores everywhere.

If you do shows, make up a noticeable and unique sign on what you are looking for. Put the cards just below the sign. You can't imagine how much business this brings! You'll get stuff brought right over to you.

---

# WANTED
# OLD WATCHES

I collect old watches.
Please take a card

 *"Sentimentality needs to go out of the window as soon as an item is up for sale. There is no value or profit justified by sentimentality."*

## Letting Go

When do you keep what you find, and when do you sell it? Here's where we start psycho-analyzing ourselves. If an item you paid $100 for is worth a thousand bucks and you have a live sale right now for it, do you sell it? Let's put it a different way. If you saw it available for sale for $1000 right now would you fork over the cash to buy it? This just might be the way to find your answer! If you'd pay that much for it, then keep it by all means, even if the amount is about the top limit of what it is worth right now. You probably like it, always wanted one, or something like that. It's okay to collect and invest. It just may grow in value.

Now if you ask, is there something else I'd rather have that's worth that amount ? If you say yes, then sell it and go get the other item!

And if you say, can I afford to buy this right now for $1000? If the answer is no and you have some debt hanging over you, sell it and enjoy the relief that profit does for you.

If you want, you can enjoy it for awhile, and sell it when the time is better, and the novelty wears off. You may eventually tire of it. You might even find that the delay could bring you a better deal. The timing may be more advantageous at a later date.

Often, you get an important item; then you will start to look around for and find similar items for sale or prices and other good information. (It's kind of like buying a new car, and you soon see dozens just like it every time you drive.) This information could be very valuable to you, if you wait. I had a wonderful antique that I bought for $850. I wasn't quite sure exactly what I found but knew it was important. It was listed for $7000. Later on I found they were selling for $13,000 to $15,000. When I was telling this to a fellow collector, he guaranteed I'd get $20,000 if I tried selling it then. Ho boy!

Once I was frustrated over whether I wanted to part with something. I really debated if I should sell the item. I finally figured it out. All I needed to do was ask myself this question, "If I had the $175 I can likely get for this item, would I spend my $175 for this item? Especially if there are other things I think I want or need?" I sold it.

Another time I traded away some items I really kind of liked. I felt just a touch of panic and sadness as I gave them up. Then I realized I had essentially sold these items for cash, and turned around and bought something I wanted even more with that cash. The only thing was, no one saw any real money—at least I felt better.

It may be easy or difficult for you to sell the prizes you find. You may be a casual collector or a hard core picker. You are probably somewhere between. If you're in it only for the money and want or need to turn your dollars or just like to hoard old junk, it's just fine.

We need collectors to create the demand and interest. We need the pickers to make their profit or they won't go out looking. We need the dealers and investors as guides to help establish the value of items. It takes all kinds.

## But It's Like Selling a Part of Myself!

Warning! Sentimental thinking!

Watch out when you're in this business for sentimentality, it can get you in trouble whether you are buying or selling. If you are at an estate sale and someone tries to justify an obviously way too high price because it's been in the family for years, it is just sentimentality. Sentimentality needs to go out of the window as soon as an item is up for sale. There is no value or profit justified by sentimentality. Historical items owned by important and famous individuals are a very different story (if you can prove or document the ownership).

One time I responded to a classified ad where an old man wanted to sell his favorite radio. (He probably bought it new as a child). When I asked what it was, and how much he wanted, he gave me an unbelievably high price. He said it was his pride and joy. (Sorry, I can't buy your memories along with it!)

## Take the Money and Run!

If you are a purely mercenary picker and have no problem selling every item you come across you won't have a problem with this topic. What if you are a collector too, and really like a whole lot of the stuff you find? Here's a rationalization exercise for you to work through when this problem comes up. (I guarantee you'll be faced with this; there is an awful lot of cool stuff out there that you'll be tempted to hold onto!)

Do you sell or keep?

**Q:** Would you rather have the money or the thing? The easy question. First think of the cash amount, now think of the item—then decide.

**Q:** If the dollars you received were then traded for the equivalent in silver coins, how big would the stack be? Now think of the item, is the silver better?

**Q:** Is the item absolutely rare and irreplaceable? Is it likely to show up again in a few months? Is it the best quality one you have ever seen?

**Q:** If you have this item and many other items you could move and liquidate, could you get one better item you'd really rather have?

**Q:** Are you investing in this item, hoping to gain a return at a later date? Can you realistically predict whether it is likely to appreciate or depreciate?

**Q:** Could you do better on a trade than you could cashing it out?

**Q:** Do you really use, study, or even enjoy and appreciate it, or is it just another conquest?

**Q:** Are you getting tired of it?

**Q:** Do you have a sale for it?

**Q:** Is that sale likely to go away?

Answer a few of these and you'll know just what to do!

## The Law of Turn Over

If you can grasp this concept, you will make more money. It's almost like understanding the law of saving money. If you do, you will have more money. Measuring turn over is a way to see how your dollars make more dollars.

Sitting with too many dollars tied up in wonderful, rare, and beautiful antiques can kill your operation. This is why various companies will have a sale. They understand they need to get the money out of the inventory. This will help them use the dollars to make more dollars. They will have close-out sales, or mark down merchandise to get the dollars out quickly. They realize it might be better to take a bath on the slow moving or dead stock. So they liquidate or convert it to cash. They use this new cash to buy faster moving items. This gives them profit.

In a nutshell, if you take a hundred dollars you invest in inventory and sell the item for $150, you made a $50 profit. If you do that four times a year, you turned that hundred dollars four times netting you $200 in profit. Can you see that if you had a faster moving item that you could turn over ten times, you would net $500 in profit!

Turn over is the secret to profit. Margin or mark-up only tells you part of the story. It tells you how much you made on one transaction. Here's another example: I buy an item for $10 and sell it for $1000. This sounds like a sweet deal, doesn't it? But, if I have 200 more of those ten dollar items in stock sitting and not selling I have still not made any profit. (200x$10=$2000) I made back $1000, but I still have $1000 of my money still tied up! Going the other extreme, if I sell them quickly, for $50 each, (much less than their $1000 list price) (200x$50=$10,000). On my original $2000 cost I made $8000 profit.

You can develop a turn-over ratio and not only make more profit, but gain happy customers too. You will have more variety and interesting things to buy.

Figuring a turn-over ratio is comparing your sales to the value of the inventory. To figure inventory turns on your overall business, use the following formula:

Beginning Inventory ..    ————
+ Purchases ...............    ————
- Ending Inventory ....    ————
/ Average Inventory  ..    ————
= Turns .....................    ————

(Average Inventory = Beginning Inventory + Ending Inventory/2)

| Examples: | A | B | C |
|---|---|---|---|
| Beginning Inventory | $2000 | $1000 | $1000 |
| + Purchases | $1000 | $1000 | $5000 |
| - Ending Inventory | $1000 | $1000 | $1000 |
| / Average Inventory | $1500 | $1000 | $1000 |
| = Turns | $1.333 (poor) | 1 (poor) | 5 (good) |

So when we look at example A above, we see that our beginning inventory is $2000, we purchased $1000, and at the end of the year we still had $1000 in inventory, giving us an average inventory of $1500. This gave us a turn-over ratio on our investment of $1000 of 1.33, which was pretty poor. You'll also notice that nothing was mentioned about how much profit margin I made. You might have any range of profit margin.

It is agreed that the higher the margin, the better. But, more importantly, your money is re-invested and at work for you. So, if I make 50% GP on a $50 item, but can sell it twelve times in that same year, it nets me $180. If I take the same item, but sell it more times during the year, it gets me more profit that I can save, spend, or re-invest. As long as I turn-over my invested dollars, I'm making money. If I hoard, I lose money. If I buy stuff that doesn't sell, I lose money. Always buy stuff that moves quickly, and then sell it!

## Same Day Service

What I really like is when I find an item and sell it on the very same day. Talk about a quick turn over! I was at a swap meet where, out of the corner of my eye, I saw an item come in on a hand truck with several other items that I quickly recognized. I immediately asked how much and was told $75. I told them "sold" and asked him to wheel it over to my space. In about an hour I re-sold the piece for $300. After thinking about it, I never even touched it with my hands!

This also works for people who have a rented showcase in an antique mall. You may see an item in another dealer's case and recognize it's potential. You see that there is a profit in the item, because the other dealer has it priced too low. Just buy it and mark it up and place it in your case. There is risk in this, but quick profit taking is possible.

## Pile it Higher and Deeper!

I have some friends who buy much of the same types of stuff as I do. In fact, I sell or trade many items with them. One problem I see them struggle with, is that they keep it all. One has a house with items everywhere in kind of a decor. He has a garage with loads of items packed to the ceiling. He used to pay good money to rent a storage unit until he wised up and built his own storage shed—but now that is full!

The other just has a storage shed he rents because he lives in an apartment. I have a shop I built adjoining my house. Yes, it is full, but I

# $ "Always buy stuff that moves quickly, and then sell it!"

move a lot of items. The inventory changes and turns over. My collection evolves. People are interesting. Some might think I'm fickle, changing my mind, deciding, and then changing what I collect and moving in a new direction later on. I guess that I just feel that we evolve.

What happens is that I learn, study new items, new technologies, and different histories and trends in items I collect. I enjoy the items, upgrade the things I eventually keep and most importantly, I profit.

Some of us pile it up. We never see the things again. We may refuse to sell anything. We want to keep it.

I was in an estate where the man had a crawl space under the entire house—no basement, just a four foot crawl space. Over the years, he piled his treasure, packing every square foot of the space. His poor daughter had to clean it all out. He put it all back there but never saw or enjoyed it again—but it was HIS. To clean out the house, she needed to rent a large commercial dumpster and actually filled it three times! There were things back in the crawl space from the 1950s that had never seen the light of day since he dragged them back there.

What happens is by keeping it all, you don't have the cash to be involved in the good deals that come up. Eventually, you start to avoid even looking at deals when you hear about them.

But too many forget that the having of an item is not nearly as enjoyable as the pursuing and obtaining of an item. I truly believe if you climb a little bit and then set your sights a little further, you will get much more satisfaction. This is one of the major benefits of a fluid collection: You absolutely enjoy it more, and by keeping it fluid you end up with better items and are in control of your wants.

You've got to sell, upgrade, give away, study, donate, throw away, buy, trade, etc. or there is no profit.

I sometimes muse that all this stuff is only cows and sheep. It used to be that a man's success was measured in how many cows or sheep or land he had in his holdings. Somehow we get comfort from having a lot of things.

If you like certain things, by all means, "Keep the best and trade off the rest." After all, you can't keep it all. You can't get it all either! If you just buy an item and see it once and put it in a box, yes, it is yours, but you enjoy it very little.

Why are we discussing this? What good does it do? First of all, I'm not trying to make you feel guilty—if in fact, you are guilty. If you recognize some of this in you, you will also see it in others you work with. You'll be a better picker if you know how it works.

Estates are filled with stuff that people bought or got and put away after seeing it once. If you display, fix, restore, use, clean, photograph, study, or document it, this will add value to it. If you trade and sell it, you enjoy the profits from it. It is exactly the same as a dividend from your investments.

If you hoard it all away, hoping or waiting for something you lose interest, you lose profit, and you lose track of it. It gets forgotten. On one hand, thank goodness others do pile it up. This means there will be a constant supply for all of us. We get to search through all of their stuff and find goodies. On the other hand, be careful yourself.

So remember, you will find some stuff that is rare and irreplaceable and very dear to your heart. Note this! (Most every deal I do includes rare, hard-to-find, classic, difficult to replace finds. This is exactly why we do it.)

It's okay to have stuff, hold it, and do things with it. It is proper to keep it for awhile, especially if it is an investment item that is likely to increase in value.

I think it's probably much easier for me to find, buy, and make good deals getting stuff than for me to sell the stuff. It's not that I am a poor salesman, it's just that I really hang onto the really neat stuff. But when I start converting it to cash, I find that is pretty neat too. There is a lot more out there than you think. If you turn it over and make wise decisions buying, you'll be wealthy in no time. (This is possible only if you reinvest the dollars in new good finds.)

## I've Got More Than You Do!

New collectors and pickers may contract a hoarding fever. If you see this in yourself, think about these things:

I've got more than you do!

1. You might start out thinking you are too late in this field and all of the good stuff is gone. Therefore, you go after anything and any quantity.
2. You seem to buy anything, in any kind of condition. You might buy at high prices and feel you're getting good deals because it will be worth more someday.
3. You always run out of money.
4. You run out of room fast.
5. You keep branching out into different fields having difficulty remembering what you want in the first place, etc.
6. It gets difficult to let go of stuff because you seem to want it all. Parts and pieces and incomplete sets are valuable to you because, "You never know when you might need these things."
7. You hang on to things because, "I think it will be difficult to ever find one of these again, they are too rare, or hard to replace."

There is hope! There might be treatment!

A. You need to let go—sell something!
B. Be somewhat mercenary.
    1. Cash always improves if your goal is to turn over your money.
    2. If you are a collector, and you sell stuff regularly, your collection will get better and better with fewer and fewer pieces as you improve and sell off. (Your focus improves).
    3. Every time you sell an item you gain contacts. Some very valuable contacts are made through buying and selling.
    4. Your growth, knowledge, and experience blossoms. Yes, you will make bad decisions, lose good deals, and sell irreplaceable goods. But you'll find and keep even more rare pieces, make and find even better deals.
    5. Overall you'll have better stuff, enjoy it more, and have the cash when you need it for the good deals which will come.
C. You need to specialize. You may want to let a few good deals slide by, unless you have a ready buyer for the goods. If you are not entirely familiar with the product, you can also be stuck.
D. "As long as you keep kicking yourself in the butt and patting yourself on the back you'll keep moving forward."
E. You need to realize the education you receive is valuable, whether it's been a profitable good deal, or a disaster. This way you are always on top.

# If You Want to Find Better Stuff, Sell Something

I guess it has to do with creating new horizons. I tried to sell a rather expensive item I had recently obtained. It was taking up quite a bit of room, and it needed to find a place to go. I tried finding someone local at first, but ended up selling the item out of state. I also ended up with lots more than the sale. One person I contacted locally, someone I haven't needed to call for many years, opened up a bigger world because of things he is now into. True, he didn't buy the item from me, but many other deals and potential deals are happening. I am so glad I called! More profit will be made from this dead end than would have been made from the original item he didn't buy from me. This is how you can get many more valuable contacts.

I guess what happens is you have a focus when you start to call around. You are asking, searching, and finding things. Because of your reason to call someone, it opens up a variety of possibilities! Look for them! As you approach new opportunities with an expectant and positive attitude, you will always accomplish more.

# Hey! Just Wholesale It!

You can spend lots of time and money and effort in trying to get top dollar for each and every item you find—or you can wholesale it!

If you decide to sell and want to lot it out, don't feel bad if you don't get full-bore retail for it. After all, you may not have wanted to do everything on our value-added list to get retail.

Yes, it is very difficult to sell an item for $40 when you know the person you sell it to will in turn sell it for $100. As a seller, if you have an opportunity to turn your money over quickly and have the cash to keep growing, it really does not matter.

Think about it:

1. You get cash in hand to buy more stuff. Cash flow justifies a business, whether it is a hobby business or a full-time business.
2. You just might buy (wholesale) items with that cash that propel you further into profit.
3. You might need the cash right now.
4. This may have been stock you have had in your inventory for a long time, not moving.
5. You may never find the right clientele to sell it for top dollar.

6. You might be tired of the item.
7. Sometimes, the buyer just really wants it.
8. You might be wishing to gain a favor with the buyer.
9. You might need the room.
10. You may have bought it for next to nothing, it's all profit.
11. Convert it in your mind into the next stuff you'll get, whether it is cash, or gold, or antiques, or debt relief. Which would you rather have? Wholesale it and move on!

# I Haven't Found a Thing Today...YIPPEE!

There's an interesting line. Let me explain. If you go out one day looking for great deals, and end up with next to nothing, it's time to celebrate. Be happy, in fact, get excited!

"Now wait a minute," you say. "I thought that this was all about finding treasures and goodies. Now you say to be happy when we're not finding good stuff?" Exactly!

We all have bad days, in fact, lots of them. You may have to run for days or even weeks with barely enough to fill half of your trunk with just so-so stuff. Be prepared for those dry spells. Realize this major point; Statistics prove that the more bad days out picking, the closer you are to the next big find. It's just like the door-to-door vacuum salesman. He would almost shout for joy every time he got a door slammed in his face, because he knew, he was literally one door closer to the person who would buy something from him. So, when you come out empty handed, GRIN!

# Liquidation Sale

By now you are very good at finding lots of stuff. Now what do you do with it? How do you make a profit? How do you turn it into cash?

Here's a few ideas:

1. Wholesale it to dealers. Establish lots of good picker/dealer relationships.
2. Sell it directly to other local collectors.
3. Put it in a booth or showcase in an antique mall.
4. Sell it at a swap meet or flea market.
5. Open up a store.
6. Go to a show specializing in your topic.
7. Advertise nationally and sell it mail order.

8. Put it on the Internet.
9. Contact a museum.
10. Place a classified ad in your local paper.
11. Swap it for faster moving merchandise.
12. Keep some of it.
13. Put notes on bulletin boards around town.
14. Tell friends (Get others to start collecting it too!)
15. Have a yard sale.
16. Contact people in your directory who specialize in the product.
17. Find other pickers for the items.
18. Make a mailing.
19. Go to a club meeting, announce what you have, or put an ad in their newsletter.
20. Have an auction.
21. Take some of it with you as you travel and contact others in that area.

Your cash flow is extremely important. If you don't have ready cash, you are effectively stopped. You don't have funds to buy in on new deals. You don't grow. The other guy gets in there and you lose out.

You need to keep this venture self-funding—that is going ahead on its own money, without investing more from household funds or from debt.

Cash is like the air you breathe. If you run out of cash, you can't pay your vendors, then your debt increases. You can't buy new stuff to sell. You also have more worry and stress which decreases motivation—then you make bad decisions.

You can have lots of great inventory and the best deals come your way. You can be the best picker in the field, but, if you run out of air to breathe, you die anyway.

You need to make a balanced activity of buying and selling and trading constantly. By selling, I mean selling and getting paid for it.

So make some plans and watch your cash flow. Use the above list, and come up with more that might be unique to your business or area. Use it to inspire you with ideas of how to turn over your inventory.

## Help Build Strong Businesses: Keep Buying!

You not only need to keep selling, but you need to balance it out with buying. Unless a body keeps eating and consuming, it dies. Unless you keep buying continually and moving your inventory, your business dies.

If you don't keep finding new and interesting items, you're not growing. If you keep buying but not selling, your business gets constipated. If you neither buy, nor sell, your network dries up, and you lose touch from the market. Then you lose interest and knowledge. A body has to be fed and move and exercise in order to grow. You have to buy and sell, trade, read, learn, discover, and meet new people on a consistent basis.

## Springboards

I wanted to buy an estate I found a while back. I didn't have the ready cash to do so, so I advertised a lot of books I had previously found. The books I had were found very reasonably, between a quarter to a dollar a piece. I ended up selling a portion of them, about 200 books for a total of $3000.

This was a healthy profit margin for me but the dealer who I sold them to made a much greater profit. I can't complain here. The reason is, that I needed the cash. The cash was to purchase another estate, which in turn, I sold for a profit. This was my springboard. Sometimes you have to take a little hit, turning your inventory over, to realize a better net profit.

## Finders' Fees or "You scratch my back, and I'll give you some money!"

After you get some good contacts and a network built up, you'll have certain individuals you know who specialize in various items. In your searches, you're bound to find some items that are highly sought after by these individuals. You may also find that the price may be out of your range or more than you are willing to risk. If you buy it, it is yours whether you sell it or not. In some cases the price is just not quite good enough to make much of a profit if you tried to sell it to the interested party.

Occasionally you can refer the item to a dealer or collector and they will reward you with a finder's fee. The finder's fee can be pretty good depending on how high it may be on their want list. This could be a percentage amount or some merchandise usually agreeable to both of you. This could actually work into a partnership as you both work and look around for items for one another and thanking each other with favors or fees.

 *"If you go out one day looking for great deals, and end up with next to nothing, it's time to celebrate."*

## The Big Score

I had an interesting situation in which I put together an estate of an engineer/collector with a sizable home full of vintage industrial equipment, which was sold to a dealer of this type of product. I received a finder's fee which included a cash amount, along with a certain lot of product I proposed before each party spoke to one another.

I was contacted inadvertently by someone about this engineer I knew, who had passed away. As we talked, I was able to persuade this contact to let me offer advise in the disposal of the estate. He was a close friend of the deceased, who I knew professionally. He was hired by the family to dispose of the goods left behind in the estate.

This was a very large estate. Not a very typical estate, it was organized by piles. Literally every room was a pile. It was unbelievable. I was able to purchase some items right off. It's always a good opportunity to buy items at a pre-estate sale. There is virtually no competition and you have time to think and not just grab!

This estate would have been fun to take lots of time going through and finding all of the treasures. The man was both a very intelligent and interesting collector. This was his life, his work and his passion. To some he was probably eccentric. I did not have the time nor the money nor the room at that point to do so. (I could not have even afforded to purchase the particular lot of product I received as finder's fee at the time!)

But I started to think. I contacted someone through an ad I saw in a professional publication. He advertises for much of the stuff I was seeing in all of these piles. I described what I saw. He asked questions. He was getting more and more excited. I was thinking. He was astute enough, because he knew through experience that the few descriptions were signs that this estate was deep in the products he deals with.

You scratch my back...

I told him I hoped there was a finder's fee involved. He assured me there was. I told him there were certain parts in the items left in the estate I wanted. He promised me if he was successful in the deal, they would be mine. He immediately got on a plane and flew here and we met at the estate. He did his deal and purchased the entire contents of the house. He rented the largest rental truck you could get, and backed it up to the house. He hired some local boys to help him load up which took two days! I got all I wanted, some thirty plus boxes and several piles of books and literature, for free! He was pleased, the estate was happy, they got cash and didn't have to work as hard removing all the stuff. I was overjoyed. There is usually a way. If you want something, you can get very creative. But then you need to watch out, because you just might get it!

## The Matchmaker Gets Paid

When you know a seller, find a buyer, and then put the two together, you are a broker. You are the middle man, or an agent. You don't buy the product. You don't sell the product. Sometimes you get a finder's fee from the buyer or you may get a commission from the seller. If you are super fortunate, you might arrange both! You may just do it for a favor or one or more parties may give you stuff because of your help.

You can be very valuable to both people. You may have built a large network of interested people in your index or directory of good contacts, because of what you have learned from this book. These contacts are your edge. As you gather your index together and contact people, and learn from them, you become a tremendous resource to others. You are now an expert. You cannot imagine the many ways things turn out. Learn as much as you can from all you meet. Take good notes.

When a situation arrives, say it's an entire estate or a collection or even a single important and valuable item; your first response is excitement. You see the item(s) and realize what is available. Clear your mind, inspect, and describe what is here. Get model numbers, brand names, and all descriptive and condition notes possible. Try and protect the material from being sold. This is next to impossible at an open public sale—you simply have to buy it. But, if this is one of those rare and exciting pre-sale opportunities you come across, you usually have the time and space to organize and protect everything. You may want to take some photographs or a video tape. Be very discreet with the buyer and seller. Be plain and up front and honest with each. Be careful to make all conditions and deals you wish for yourself plainly known before any introductions are made.

If you see it is a good match and you are a good negotiator, you can probably make out very well without having spent a dime or handling any of the product.

As you're conversing with one person and then the next, you may be tempted to give each a little "G2" on the other person. By "G2" I mean subtle information like, "I know he's got the money to spend..." or, "This guy is hoping to get an amount of $... for this stuff." This is OK as long as you are honest and don't break confidences. After all you are the ambassador and a liaison and agent between the two. You are representing the other person in the initial stages of the deal. It's an interesting and literally, rewarding experience!

What is really fun is the three-way deal. You get something, he gets something, I get something. What a blast!

Did you really think that a small classified ad you noticed, cut out and pasted in your index would pay off that big? Do you now understand how if you are organized, and catalog your contacts, this gives you an edge among all of the other pickers?

## Brokering, a Classic Classified Ad Story

I saw an advertisement in a magazine that got me thinking. It was simply a person who wanted a certain type of watch. Not a rare watch, just one of those older style electronic watches that light up, you know, with light emitting diodes or LED display. They went out of style as LCD displays became more perfected and cheaper to make.

I also knew a small service and sales company that used to sell and repair all kinds of these watches. I thought that he might have a box of defective old watches he'd let go cheap. Nope, he didn't have much in the defective stuff, but he happened to have thirty brand new in original boxes, old stock LED watches. We negotiated a price of $10 a piece for the watches. As I contacted the collector who placed the ad, we then decided that $25 each would work for both of us. (I have no idea what he sold them for!)

I asked him to send me a cashier's check for the amount and then I would pack up and send him the watches.

I realized $450 in quick profit from reading one ad and making one phone call. I could then use the cash on something else. Gosh, this is better than the stock market!

# Negotiating Secrets!

Here I go, I'm giving away some of my negotiating secrets. You may think initially that once it is printed, these tips won't work. I am not concerned, and I'm the one giving away the secrets!

First of all, I'm sorry to say, not everyone will have a chance to read this book. Also, everyone's style, manners, and delivery is different. Plus, every deal and situation will change, so it keeps working even if two people read the same tips and try it on each other! Much of what is said and done in a negotiation becomes subconscious and second nature. You won't even be aware you're using these techniques.

As you learn things that are useful to you in this book, you will try and succeed and sometimes fail. You will adapt and change and get better. In time, I know I will come up with some new ones, and so will you.

**Secret:** When negotiating, watch and remember what the other person says and does. He or she might be a master and your negotiations on the deal might not go as well, but you will learn much if you watch, and remember, and do like he or she does next time on a different deal. Take good notes.

# Secret: Selling to Someone

If someone offers me $35 for an item I was hoping to get $15 for, I usually hesitate and think about it. I might even make a few statements about the item or pick it up and play with it or something. Then I finally agree. If you get all excited, and say, "Well yessir, I can get some more if you want," then something is suspicious. Your customer feels he went too high and just might change his mind. At the very least, he'll feel bad. The best negotiating is when both parties feel good.

If the $35 is lower than what I hoped to sell it for, I might say, "Oh no, you know, I paid more than that to get it myself." Or, even better, "If I saw one today for sale for $35, I'd buy it myself! I think I'd rather keep it for that price."

If the situation is such that you can get them to "toss something else in on the deal", here's your chance. You may have seen something of theirs that you want, just waiting for them to want something you have.

Or, how about this, "Well, that thing is something I've even considered keeping, I only really brought it along in hopes that someone really wanted it badly, and made me an offer I couldn't refuse."

You can simply say, "No, you'll have to do better."

Never tell them you are hurting financially. They just may tempt you with some mediocre wholesale offer, knowing that you'll finally succumb to the dollars and walk away in effect stealing the item from you!

As you can, especially if they are buying many items from you, you might try to give them some extra items for free. These can be surplus, common or similar things they may have had shown some interest in but you consider of little value. Your customer will feel like they received a killer deal, and you get rid of dead inventory.

Negotiating is fun and actually makes you feel better. Let's look at an example:

If you are trying to sell an antique player piano and tell the price to someone who is interested, let's say $500. If this person immediately says, "Sold!" you will probably ponder afterward for a long time, "Gee, I probably could have got a whole lot more for it."

Now if your customer looks at it up and down, tries it out, checks around and finally says, "The best I'd probably give you is $400." You may even say, "No, I need at least $450," and then at some point the deal is done at $450. He goes home smiling and thinking, "I did great, I talked him down $50."

You may be thinking, "Well, that's probably all it's worth, I'm sure glad I was able to get that much for it, plus actually talk him up the extra $50." You go away counting your cool $350 profit, and he goes on his way dreaming of how he'll fix it up and get $1000 for it. You are both very pleased. This was a good deal.

Don't go down in price and stick to your guns when you can see in his eyes that he really wants it and is maybe even obsessed. You're there to squeeze every penny out of the deal. He'll go away with his buy, always wondering if you took advantage of him. He'll maybe even tell his friends—you'll never know.

You can call it bargaining, haggling, negotiating, selling, buying. If done with an open mind, and a good attitude, you'll learn, you'll profit, you'll gain customers and friends. You'll even enjoy it because everybody is a winner.

Isn't it interesting how much business isn't done this way. We go to the grocery store or department store and shop. That is, if the price is too high we may or may not keep looking until finding it cheaper, never bothering to try and get a better deal. (Can you imagine haggling for 25¢ over a carton of ice cream?) If we just pay the price, we either are numb to the bad deal and go on, or get astonished and just complain about how hard it is to live in these times.

Some negotiators are weasels. They do it with poor form. Some just complain their way through it, beg a lot, or act as if they're stupid to try and get your pity. There are also those who, because you want something, all of a sudden decide what they have is made out of gold. You could most likely find similar items just about anywhere; in fact, you do. But, because you want it, it's now very valuable... (just walk away).

## Good Negotiating Phrases to Memorize:

1. "I don't usually pay that much for them when I find them." (Infers you see them around all the time for better prices, and they better lower their price if they want to sell it to you now.)
2. "I usually try and pay a lot less for my first one, because if I do find another one, I will have to pay a lot more to complete the pair."
3. "Most [watches, radios, etc.,] are very inexpensive, that's why I like them." (I mean, what can you say to that line. Hey, it worked on me!)
4. "What about if I throw in an extra ($20, or another widget, or...) to sweeten the deal?"
5. "I'd like to get that much for it; I guess it's because I really like the looks of it myself." (Uh-oh! They have competition breathing down their neck, and it's you! or–They offer you a price below that which you want.)

"You know what? I'd probably buy it for that price, too, if I saw another one right now, sorry," or "No, I don't think so, for that price I'd just as soon keep it for myself."

## Negotiating Checklist

1. Always negotiate.
2. Be creative. There just might be a way. In fact, expect you'll make the deal!
3. Research first!
4. Remember that both of you should always win.
5. Watch out for pride and ego.
6. Don't talk too much. Know when to shut up.
7. Play it out in your mind that it works before you start. Take both sides.
8. Determine your lowest acceptable deal up front.
9. Set a goal of what you want most before you begin.
10. Watch and learn from the techniques and strategy they use!

11.  Write it out on paper. How does it turn out?
12.  Never give control to the other party.
13.  Never assume that the price is fixed.
14.  Be open minded and listen to the other side.
15.  They might give more than you hoped for.
16.  Don't burn bridges. You want a good relationship in the future.
17.  Never go into a negotiation assuming you won't get what you want.
18.  Sometimes it just doesn't happen—**WALK AWAY**.

Practice these things. Try them out and you will perfect your skills. Develop other strategies and add to the list. Remember, it never hurts to ask!

## The Big Negotiation

The more hopeful, emotional, and excited you are, the more you'll pay for it.

This payment can take different forms. It can be more cash. It can be that you give much more in trade to sweeten the deal. It could also be that you gave up or overlooked certain flaws in order to just have it but will be sorry about later.

Your side of the negotiation is hindered by your wants. Now want, in itself, is okay. You need to have wants, wishes and goals, or this stuff doesn't work. But too much want flips into greed or obsession which will negatively influence your decisions.

You may know that an item you are pursuing is very valuable. Let's just say it is worth $1000. You may have some items with a similar value. You know they cost you very little. This might be a good trade, and an easy negotiation.

If you perceive that the other person will probably do anything to get what you have, then you usually do very well in the trade. So it is obvious that if you show signs of excitement and want (or absolute lust) then you are very vulnerable. Here's a good reason in itself for us to not covet our neighbor's goods!

So a good poker face is useful. If you are somewhat aloof, indecisive or have genuine indifference, it will help you. This goes for either buying or selling or trading negotiations.

Here's another example, the thing you want to sell is marked $300. The fellow says, "I'll give you $100 for it." Your answer, if in an anxious state of mind would be, "Well, um, gosh, mister, I marked it $300." If you have a controlled answer, not caring if the guy buys it from you or not you might say, "$100! No, that's too low. I'd rather keep the thing for $100. In fact, if I saw another one right now I'd sure pick it up for a hundred bucks." Who's in better control?

Or, if buying something you ask, "So how much do you want for those...." He says, "$100 each." You answer, "No thank you, I usually don't pick those up unless they are cheap. I'll buy them if I see them for $40 or $50 tops." Now you are saying a couple things—you are inferring that you are some sort of a dealer, and you need to buy wholesale. After all, you may in fact, sell those retail for $100 too. You are also inferring you have in the past looked away when you saw them priced before at his price. He may worry that he won't possibly sell them at his price. You have to be willing to walk away from deals. You can't afford to pay retail if you are reselling.

When trading, you are actually shopping. Look around at the stuff as if you are shopping with cash. Place it in a pile or make a list. Tell the seller exactly what you would like. Show him what you have. Put it like this, "For my stuff, which of the items selected will you let me have?" Hopefully you selected good things and several of which would satisfy the deal. He may remove a couple of items from his side. The next stage is to say, "Okay, if I toss in another three widgets, will you let me have those items?" More often than not this worked for me!

Enjoy trading! Have fun! Try to trade up, then go trade up again with someone else. Make a list afterward of what you gave and what you got. Put retail values to the list and see how you do. Learn from it for next time.

You will also learn a whole lot about the other person's wants. You can almost go shopping for this person, when out picking. You have a customer for certain types of product now.

When you are asked by a potential customer, be ready to answer the question you will be asked. "So, do you have any idea how much you want for it?" (your item). Always be very ready with a "yes" and then state, confidently your price. Hopefully you have researched the price by then, or know your stuff and can place a current value on it. You often will get what you ask.

If you hem & haw, he realizes you don't have a clue. If you are not ready to sell, tell him you need to do some more research first. I asked a dealer once after the deal was done how he came up with the price he asked. He said, "Well, I priced it based only on the appeal it had to me."

## Making the Big Offer

So you found something you want to buy or you may be negotiating the purchase of an estate. Here are some things to keep in mind as you make your offer:

1. Find any defects in the product and point them out to the seller.
2. Communicate your experiences in buying the same items elsewhere if appropriate.
3. It's always better to find their price out before you make any offer. More often than not it's lower than you would have been happy to pay.
4. You may need to explain how the value to dealers (you) differs than the value to an end collector. You typically need to make at least 50% of the list price on something you sell. Besides you will be expected many times to have to give your buyer a discount.
5. Let the seller know how you are willing to buy the entire lot, good and bad. Explain that there is usually a whole lot of left over stuff that is unsalable junk. Yes, it may have some value, but you won't get much for it.
6. You are also taking a chance. There is a risk in time and money for you. Also explain your expenses involved.
7. What if they see a catalog with high prices on stuff like they hope to sell to you? There are those large catalog houses who do sell the items for higher prices, but realize they also offer lots of different services. They have expensive advertising to deal with. They also have the luxury of thousands of eyes seeing their ads. They have a much greater chance of finding someone, somewhere, that will pay their high price.

## Dickering

The best advice I can give here is, "It doesn't hurt to ask...be bold!" The worst thing they can say is, "forget it!" If you are kind, convincing, and have a friendly attitude, many times you can buy at the better price.

**Tip:** If you hang around a sale, you will hear all sorts of good approaches used by other experienced pickers and savvy buyers. There will be all kinds of good approaches and negotiation techniques and strategies used you can learn. You can also find out quickly which techniques won't work at that particular sale.

Incidentally, at sales of all kinds you will see firsthand who the people are, and what types of things they are interested in. This is a great place to make exceptional contacts! You hear someone say, "Do you happen to have any old fountain pens?" So then you may wish to approach that person, ask for a card, and say you'll keep an eye out for fountain pens for them. Write down particulars about what they like, dislike, etc. Learn from them! Tell them what you look for, and give them your card. If they have no interest in your things, they might be very helpful and tell you where they think they might be found, giving you some good leads and haunts to check out. This is perfect networking. I guarantee it has great payoffs!

Be friendly with the other shoppers. So much of the time we get afraid to talk, for fear that everybody is our competition. In a way they are, but in a way, everybody is a resource too! They may turn out to be very good customers. You can gain so very much more by communicating and making good friends and contacts, than by what you might lose at the one sale you are at right now. Everybody has different timing or places they travel to check out. Everyone has ideas and hunches that are unique. Different pickers have varied interests, but their knowing what you like will benefit you in the end, as you now have more eyes and ears looking around for you. You'll be absolutely amazed what kind of a network of good contacts you'll build, whether it's for tips, good leads or buying and selling both to and from them.

What's interesting is you will also overhear of these peoples' latest deals, where they are, and how they found out about them. You hear about people and dealers to stay away from. You are right in the thick of it and can learn a lot.

## Collector's Curse
## (You want it? You pay the price...now!)

The man said he learned a valuable lesson. If you see a great piece, a very important and valuable piece—one of those once-in-a-lifetime items you know you will never, ever get a chance to buy again—you never lowball bid on it. You keep laying down the money until you can take it away. The value of an item like that now becomes what you paid for it. I had a very big dealer in expensive quality pieces tell me on rare items, whatever your seller wants to sell it for—you pay it!

Now your knowing this as a "dealer" will help you, if you ever have a chance at a major item. Realize you will get the price you want. Don't let

The fine art of conversation...

it go for a song. Don't fret, wondering if you will ever get your money out of it. The high-end, high-quality and very expensive items always have a buyer.

## He's Mine!

Say you have an item you sell or buy by the pound. The buyer might look at the box or pile and say, "I'll give you $200 for it." Your next statement should be something like "But there's fifty lbs. there." (Here's the secret: you might not even know what the stuff is or what it's worth, but your exclaiming, "It's fifty lbs. there," infers you know what is there and what it's worth. It also gives a signal to the buyer that they have another chance to buy it if they raise the price, especially if they know it's worth a lot more). If it isn't worth much more, the buyer will probably tell you.

Let's put it differently. If he asks, "How many pounds are there?" and you say, "Gosh, I have no idea." He's now thinking, "He's mine! I can offer anything I want!" This works both ways, so be careful.

## The Fine Art of Conversation (or) "Shut Up!"

Sometime you'll find out that you will do some swapping or buying or selling and realize you blew the deal because you kept talking. When the deal is done, stop.

You may be negotiating and even finalize a very fine trade when then you say something, and you wish your hand could fly out of your mouth after the words. I've done it.

I knew a salesman who was very capable, very technical, and had a great personality. He could usually handle any situation with ease and really knew his stuff. The problem was he wanted to tell you all that good stuff he knew. He almost lost some good business because of it. The store where I worked received comments from customers annoyed by him and even asked us not have him come by anymore. I've done it to myself more than once, eventually giving back product when I really didn't need to, or leaving dollars on the table or any number of things.

This does not mean if you hope to sweeten a deal for someone by giving a little extra that you need to stop. No, if you intend to make your customer happy on purpose, that's wonderful; it will eventually come back to you.

Or, if you need to make a bad deal right, and need to give back product or dollars, this is good too. Make your customer happy by all means. When I was buying a 1940s vintage truck from a co-worker once, he asked, "Want to make me an offer?" I said, "How about a hundred bucks?" He said, "How about forty!"

# Ca$h is Good!

When you pay cash for an item, it's good for a couple of reasons. First, it is a great incentive. People like cash and may be willing to do a better deal for cash money. They may worry about checks, especially from strangers.

Cash is also good for a level of anonymity. They won't call you back, changing their mind, etc. You don't get all the questions day after day it seems, when you keep yourself anonymous. After all, they don't know who to call.

This is a cash business. You have to keep it fluid. You need to have plenty to buy stuff. And you have to get it when you sell stuff. Watch out for credit. Don't take it, don't give it. When you owe money it seems the month only lasts for a few days and the payment time is here again, Dang! When someone owes you money it seems that weeks turn into months and months (if you ever do get paid).

# Trading up

If you have a quantity of some lesser value items and are able to trade for one better, higher valued or nicer item (usually equal to or even higher to the combined value of all of your stuff), this is trading up. Trading up for you is usually a good deal if you know the stuff you're dealing in. Trading down isn't always a good idea, unless you know you can quickly turn it for cash and it was very advantageous for you to do so.

# Advantages:

1. You may have a hard time normally selling all of the lesser value items as readily as the higher value item.
2. The higher value item probably excites you more!
3. You probably have more value even if it was a straight dollar for dollar trade because you may have had to make deeper discounts on many of the lower value items to eventually get rid of them separately.

The joy of trading!

4. There is some inherent liquidity in larger ticket items, as serious collectors like the big important stuff, although it might take a while.

5. You can now have a higher plateau to trade up even higher by using this one item—much further than you could have, with the previous lot of products.

6. Remember the statement, "One man's trash is another man's treasure...er... stuff."

7. One item takes up less room than several items.

If you are a collector, the process of trading up means your collection is getting refined with better and fewer items. You'll end up with a high value, high quality, fine collection.

If you are a dealer, this means your inventory is gathering better and higher end stock. Your reputation improves. You might find that you don't need to spend as much time and energy selling one piece vs. many.

Remember it may be a good idea to toss in more lower value items in your trade up. Your customer always feels better if you sweeten the deal. Cash can always be used as part of a trade, both on his side or yours. This is especially an incentive if what you want is really outstanding or if the items you are disposing of are slow-moving products.

## The Joy of Trading

I really like to trade. It is like going to a store and having a shopping spree. You get to buy just about anything you want without spending any cash! Most of the time the other person feels he is high grading you and all the while you feel you are high grading him!

Look for items that have a high trade value or can be used as currency. Some collectibles you'll find have a steady value and can be used just like dollars when looking for products you wish to trade for.

It's usually a good idea at the end of the trade, to give up one more item, after he and you got what you both want. This makes him feel good about the trade and about you. We've all heard horror stories for people who feel they have been burned by someone in a trade. They will never swap or have dealings with them again. They also tell their friends. Don't let this happen to you. A bad reputation can kill your business. A good reputation will help you succeed.

# Chapter 7:

# Book Picking –A Unique Career

# Book Scouts

For some reason, some dealers call book pickers, scouts. It must be because of the specific nature of book picking and the search that the dealers have is targeted to certain titles, authors, or editions.

Book picking seems to be in a major class by itself. First of all, book collectors are a very passionate and dedicated sort of people. Book collecting is also probably more of an accepted obsession. Think about it, everyone loves good books. I even love the smell of old books! A library is acceptable to have. People love to come in and see what books you have on the shelf. Other hobbies and collections sometimes raise eyebrows even though they might be pretty interesting. Esoteric is the word.

You'd have to be involved to understand the reasoning and drive—but not books. Books are a safe kind of passion. Many people even in the general population have very collectible and even some rare books in their homes.

Book collectors may start with a certain specialty and easily branch into other various topics that naturally connect to their original topic, this is very easy to do. The result is a constantly growing library. Serious bookmen get pretty competitive and secretive and protective of their passion. Some are very aggressive collectors as they fulfill their need to obtain books. Some feel the day is utterly wasted if they go out and don't bring back an armful or box filled with books. Many book pickers pick for themselves first and then scout for various dealers to pay for their hobby.

Never overlook books when you are out searching for other goods. Start your own library or at least find what books are sought after. You'll likely be in the same places the books are when you seek collectibles and antiques. You might as well get the books, too. You can always find a buyer for good books.

Talk to others who you see picking books all the time. Although they are your competition you can still find out a lot by asking questions. They will tell you who the dealers are that you can sell certain topics to. They will warn you of certain individuals. You might even make a good supplier or customer from these people you meet.

You can learn what's hot, as they brag about certain finds they made out on. They will tell you how cheap they found something and how much they got for it! Many love to boast. Ask them how they arrive at certain prices, and they may tell you. A lot of them just use other dealer's catalogs to obtain their prices. Others use recent auction reports to base pricing. Just by shooting the breeze with some of these folks, you can gain tons of good information.

I was watching a professional book scout one day. I have seen her pick books many times. One day I thought I'd just watch her pick as they wheeled out a new cart of books at a large thrift store. As I came up to the cart this time, I was probably more interested in how she worked the cart than in looking for books myself. She worked it well. She first scans quick, grabbing and not even looking closely at what she has. At this point, condition, date of printing, first editions, signed copies, or even the price of the book is of no concern. It's just get it off the cart and away from any exposure to the competition.

In mining, it's just mucking out the ore. High-grading comes later. She grabbed up all she could grab quickly and hold in her arms. When it was safe, she reached for a shopping cart, and now had time to scan each shelf at least two or three times. This was a fine tuning effort, which I noticed, rendered some good titles. At this point, she took the time to open the books to inspect for better value.

I kind of felt I must have been a real pain to be there hovering and watching her work. I was so fascinated in what I was seeing, I even noticed I was smiling as I watched her techniques. After the cart was inspected entirely, she then high-graded what she found, and I'm sure she returned some to the cart. Her stack had twenty or thirty books—I had one. She knew what she wanted, knew several places to sell them, and knew the prices. Of course, her interests and market vary from mine, and I would not have wanted most of what I saw in her stack. However, she wanted them, and just may have found some valuable pieces today. I'll bet you that if I knew more of the market I would have wanted them!

## Corruption, Ethics, and Sneaky, Clever People

As you get into book picking, it just may become obvious how serious some book scouts and dealers are. You may see the same people at the same places all the time, and after awhile it seems they know when and where the good books are going to be. I've been told by book collectors that because of the fervor and competition in the book field, many times there are back door deals that happen even in the best of places.

Library sales try and keep their sales above board as much as possible. Some even try and hold preview sales for their most anxious supporters. They charge a little more at the preview sales, but it is usually worth it.

The problem happens when the volunteers hide books. Sometimes they will stack them behind other books or in areas that are unlikely for people to look and then notify their culprit friends where to look when they arrive at the sale.

Thrift stores put out books at various times, and those who are pros

Beware of sneaky, clever people!

can almost determine a schedule of when new loads come out. This is fine; those who are organized, able to schedule their time, and work hard deserve what they get. It's bad when they get a call from an insider who notifies them of the next load or where in the cart the best ones are, so they are always first. A regular guy doesn't have a chance.

Usually at an estate sale it's anything goes. If you get to the estate sale first, or even the day everyone else, more power to you. Creativity plays a good role here. I really don't think being fair is a real concern here. However, those who steal or fake prices are at fault. If you are early, it's okay. The early bird gets the worm. After all, the estate wants to dispose of the stuff anyway they can.

Ethics has gray areas.

Some pickers get very bad reputations and are very disliked by some of the stores they hang out at. One day I went to a large local thrift store. I asked about some particular books I was looking for, and to my surprise, I was invited back in the back room. I was able to see and choose many books before they were put out on the floor. It was mainly because they were so upset with some other pickers who were a real thorn in their side. Apparently, they are rude and abusive. They even knock you over as the doors are opened in the morning, knocking stuff over all the way back to the stacks. This upset them, and so they invited me to go back first. Gray area, maybe, but not as bad as treating the employees and other customers rudely.

Pick for the fun and excitement. Do it for collecting and for helping your income. Consider it investing, but never do it for greed. Those who do are very obvious. It is apparent why and how they operate. I really think if you have the right reasons and work hard and are nice to others, it comes back to you. Work smarter, not meaner.

As you get more and more involved in book picking, you will begin to get a good nose for the best old books. I guess this is why I like the smell of them.

## Conversation With a Book Dealer about Pickers

Let's just call him George, the book dealer. He has a wonderful little used book store in a strip mall in town. He sells all subjects. He is a very nice guy. He is happy, successful, and enjoys what he does.

I asked George about pickers. He says he has two pickers. The rest of his books come in on trade from regular folks. These pickers know what

George wants and they know what he specializes in. They know what he pays for books. He buys just about every title they bring him. (They know their subjects well, and what George's customers want). They get cash or sometimes trade for what they bring in. It was also interesting to see that one of George's pickers was a literature professor at a local university. Pickers are all sorts of people.

George gets mad at collectors who come in saying "This book lists at such and such a price in the book valuation guides, I sell it to you for..." He sends them out the door. His pickers find good stuff, make a profit, and George gets a good deal. George makes a profit. It's a relationship.

# Chapter 8:

# Dealing with the Stuff

## Price Guides

Price guides are only that, a guide. They are not price books or catalogs like various industries use to set retail or even wholesale prices. You'll get an idea of a value for an item based upon all kinds of reasons. Some prices may be listed based upon prices the author saw it advertised for. Some may be what it was priced at in a store (whether or not it was sold).

Prices can have big swings based on geographic areas. Your town might be in a deprived area for certain items, and the price could be very high. In a different city, the same item could be way low because they're found everywhere and nobody wants them because they are hard to sell.

Prices are also as fickle as the people that buy the stuff. Demand goes up and down. News on a certain item, in a magazine article, or at a major show can send buyers walking away or scrambling and frothing at the mouth, trying to locate something. You have to be involved to follow these trends. One day it's certain styles. Next it's color or brand name that drives it up or down.

Price guides are important, very important. They have pictures, model numbers, and historical documentation. They often include finding tips or quality hints that are extremely valuable. The description and listed information can be very helpful as well as interesting reading if it is something you are really into. Plus, the beginner, as well as the expert, can use the ballpark prices listed as a guide to help them when buying, selling and swapping stuff. It makes a good starting place for negotiations. Price, after all, is really the amount you can sell it for anyway. Obtain all the price guides and histories on products you focus on and other areas that catch your interest. The guides are a good reference.

## Picker's Workshop: Make Your Own Price Guide

In just about any field of collectable, you will find a group of related items that have no official price guide. This can be frustrating, especially if you are new to the market. You may feel that "something is going on" and you don't get it. You feel naive and left out. Some collectors that fervently seek these items know the models and styles and values—you are clueless.

You need to start building your own price guide. Get a stack of Rolodex cards and keep them handy as you read articles and ads, and as you shop. Jot down model numbers and the prices things are selling for. The more information you gather, the better.

Price Guides

Item type, brand name, model number, and price or value are the minimum information. Books would include notes such as title, author, date, etc. As you place the cards in your Rolodex file, you can sort by item, i.e. books, toys, radios, etc. You can start with the obscure types and then fill in later with the common things. Sort them alphabetically by brand and then model number in the rolodex file. Later on you could computerize if you desire. It does not matter that you duplicate similar models. In fact, it is preferred that you follow trends and get average selling prices. In a very quick time, you will have assembled a valuable and useful price catalog. More important, you'll start to see the trends in pricing and be able to keep up with the pros.

This guide, as with any price guide is just a starting place, a reference. "Your mileage and price may vary...."

## Trick of the Trade: Just Try and Buy One

Sometimes you find something that you think might be particularly valuable, but you don't have anything that gives you a value. One way to find out is to try and buy one!

Call up someone who specializes in what the item is and ask if they have one for sale. If they do, ask how much. If they don't, ask if they know where you can find one. If it is quite rare, they'll tell you. You could ask then, "So, if I ever did have a chance to buy one, just how much would I expect to pay for it?" You'll probably find a close approximation to the fair market value of the item. You could then call around if you want to get a better average from those who know. You never have to tell them you have one on hand—you're just shopping. Playing dumb may help you here, too.

Now, locally, be very careful. You should already have the item in your possession, or have a good lock on it. You might be calling a local dealer to get information who is working the same deal! If he gets wind of or suspects you are after the same item, he'll quickly go and try to finalize the deal. In the meantime, he may try and give you erroneous information to throw you off course!

## Putting a Price on Your Priceless Discoveries

Figuring selling prices.

First, you need to realize there are many stages of price. You need to understand and differentiate between them.

**List price or retail.** This is the price it sells for in a store, usually to the end user customer, or collector. It books for this price; that is, this is what the price guides list at. This is about the limit the market will bear.

**Dealer cost or dealer price.** Typically 1/2 or 1/3 of list price. If you sell or wholesale to dealers, this is what they pay and how much you get.

**Collector-to-collector price.** Yes, collectors sell among themselves. This is par with the dealer cost. Pretty close to the value something is really worth.

**Picker price.** Much of the time you will find stuff at ten cents on the dollar or better. This is how much you buy stuff for when you are out foraging at the sales.

**Free.** It happens!

You will be involved with all of these prices. You profit by wholesaling to dealers, selling to collectors, and even sell or trade at retail values. Try not to get too hung up on where the deal is on the scale—as long as you turn your inventory and make a profit.

Everyone hopes to buy low and sell high. Some deals are unbelievably profitable, but some you lose on too. The main goal should be to just keep finding better sources, contacts, and customers. Always be looking for better stuff. You can always make more money by turning your inventory than by trying to get your highest dollar out of every find.

When you have an item to sell, there is a lot to think about. There are many different factors that can affect the price. There are also many factors you might feel could affect the price but have no real bearing on the value of the object.

**1. Are you emotionally attached, in any way to the item?**

If you are attached emotionally, watch out! You will probably ask too much for the item, and not be able to sell it. If it belonged to a deceased parent, or your best friend gave it to you, or it was a Christmas present from your first-born child, to someone else that means nothing—no one else has the bonded value you feel.

**2. Is it historically significant? Do you have proof or documentation?**

Now here's where those bonding values do reach out to others. The item may have a story. It may have been used in a movie. The thing was previously owned by a celebrity. Maybe it is a prototype unit handmade by the inventor. Guess what, You still have to watch out! It could be a fake. You might not be able to prove the previous ownership. Hearsay doesn't last. You need documentation, signatures, letters, photos and other proof. With such documentation, the value can be much higher.

*"Sometimes you find something that you think might be particularly valuable, but you don't have anything that gives you a value. One way to find out is to try and buy one!"*

## 3. Has it been repaired or restored. Is it worn and used, or is it in perfect mint condition?

You need to inspect the items you buy and sell for cracks, errors, repairs, and fakery. Be careful when you buy, and be up front and disclose all you know when you sell. It is horrible to sell an item, and later find out the buyer wants to return it because you weren't clear on a description. The best thing is to sell as is, as found, untested. Don't try and pass off obvious errors.

## 4. Is the item common?

Commonly found products won't bring the value rare items will. Some very good products, and very nice antiques are common and have low values. Sometimes these low values are regional. Sometimes they are hard to find in other areas of the country or even different countries and demand higher prices.

## 5. Is the item old, classic, or becoming vintage? Could it be a pre-collectible?

Certain items do have a lot of potential for future collectible products. Savvy investors can do well if they choose these items and tuck some away in hopes for collectible values. Be careful.

## 6. Is it the right color? Is it aesthetic or pleasing to look at? Is it kind of funky or wild and interesting to look at?

Old antiques are interesting and beautiful and have classic lines. They are pleasing to the eye. They were made by craftsmen and the art is lost. Then the "Deco" items were stretching the art and have "a look" that is very interesting and sought after. The 50s have a kind of crazy look and feel that the baby boomers remember.

These styles have to be learned and recognized. You almost kind of have to "get into it." Once you understand, you can pick it out and have a better feel for the values and prices as you buy and sell.

### 7. Do you like it? What would you pay for it? (What did you pay for it?)

As a consumer, you can tell a lot about prices. Sometimes you just have to price it based on a gut feeling or by the value it has to you.

### 8. Do you have an abundance in your inventory? Is it something easy or difficult for you to sell? Would you like to dispose of the material? Do you need the cash?

These are reasons to take less profit and price lower.

### 9. Do you have a ready clientele that will buy this product anytime you find it?

If so, you can usually set your price, but be careful you don't upset the deal by taking advantage of them. You stand to lose if you are greedy. Note: Real serious collectors realize you have to put your dollars down and buy it.

### 10. Has there been a favorable write up in a national magazine or book on your item? Has it been the feature product in a major collector's show?

Usually this is an opportunity to take advantage of a bit more profit on the product. Interest is piqued. Demand is high. It's famous.

### 11. Do you know much about the product?

If you don't, about all you can do is copy prices you have seen elsewhere and hope they are right. Or take the time to study the market and learn more about what you have. If it is a rare and important piece, maybe an appraisal is in order.

### 12. What are others selling them for in your area?

Regional values will vary greatly. East coast, West coast, all areas have a different supply and demand. Some areas might have a larger supply of an item because it was produced there. However, demand might be higher because the historical significance is greater there too. Many collectors in that area may have worked at the manufacturer, or had parents work there, etc. They may specialize in that particular brand, etc. Compare with the national market price if possible.

## 13. Is there a way to get some sort of an official appraisal on the item?

Sometimes you can get an appraisal by asking the right questions. For example, you can take the approach that you are looking to buy an item and ask, "How much would I have to pay for one of these if I found one?" If you ask this of enough dealers, you might get a good idea of the value of the item.

An official appraisal by a qualified and honest person will usually cost you something. Always get it in writing on their letterhead and attach all of your documentation, photos, etc.

## 14. Have you noticed some appreciation or depreciation in the product in the current market?

If prices are sliding, it might be well to investigate and maybe dump what you can now. If the prices are climbing, hold onto what you have as an investment.

Here are some things that can affect an item's worth:
condition
authenticity
documentation
proof
previous owner
needs of seller
want of buyer
hype
market value
advertised value
prestige & status
rarity
historical importance
investment
value
supply and demand
competition
value added
quality
beauty
aesthetics
model type
prototype
ability to pay
Other steps helpful in evaluating something you have found;

First of all you need to identify the item. Look for brand names, model numbers, etc. Also note that certain colors and styles do make quite a bit of difference in values. See if there is a price guide available on the products. You may even need to research it in the original manufacturer's literature. Try and find an expert.

Many times just calling a dealer or two can help you find who's the most knowledgeable collector in the field. Some magazines have extensive classifieds, which have for sale and wanted advertisements that can help you make valuations. Auction reports can also list same or similar products and the prices they were sold for. Some dealers send out catalogs and lists containing prices of items they wish to sell. These can be helpful to compare for current market prices.

Remember that condition has the biggest effect on pricing.

When you go to sell the item, you should ask yourself a few questions:

How quick do I need to sell this product?

Did I buy it right? (Did I get a good deal?)

What is my overhead?

Will I likely need to give my customer a discount? (If so, pad the price a bit, to come down).

Do I like the item?

Has it been kicking around in my inventory for a long time?

If sold, is there something else I need the money quickly for?

Does my customer really just have to have it? (price goes up)

On the other hand, sometimes you just have to take your best offer, even if it isn't as good as you originally hoped for. If you have had something for a long time, and have no other offers, the bird in the hand may be your best bet.

Don't get hung up on the price. There are many prices. There's your cost. There's wholesale prices. The current market also has a certain value or price. There is the asking price and the actual selling price.

## Pre-Collectibles

Pre-collectibles are a risky but potentially interesting and lucrative business. Let's look at a scale of time as it might relate to antiques and collectible items:

1. Antiquities (prehistoric artifacts).
2. Antiques—over 100 years old.
3. Antiques—less than 100 years old.
4. Collectibles—fairly recent, memorabilia, nostalgia.
5. Pre-collectible—recent items, no real trend yet, but interesting.

If you can predict or foresee an item or group of products as classics, potentially collectible, or sleepers, you might just be able to cash in on a pre-collectible. You may be able to corner the market on items now while people are throwing them away—before they get hot.

The key is to find items that have just gone out of style or are being replaced by newer, better products. The usefulness is gone. It might be very readily available now at low prices and in quantity. Nobody is buying and there is no interest. Look for innovative items, for example, the first new type of toy. But watch out—it might never take off. You might have all your money tied up in a warehouse of garbage.

Realize that if stuff is now showing up at sales and swaps very cheap, it also means a much larger quantity is being tossed into the garbage. This disposal might be to some a disaster, but in reality, gives increasing value to the items left.

Some fairly recent examples that may have surprised some people include:

Miniature reel-to-reel tape recorders

LED watches

Electronic pocket calculators

These were somewhat recently considered junk but now can be very valuable. Isn't this absolutely amazing!

Realize that some seem to have a vision of what will be a collectible. They may have some forceful influence in how the market grows. It very well could be that they drive the interest to where it is. First they collect, then hoard, document, write newsletters, start clubs, establish prices, and even print books on the subject. Many interesting stories are written, wanted classified ads start showing up, museums are formed, then feverish trading builds the craze.

Unbelievable prices start being quoted. Before you know it, these items are a full-blown collectible. Soon others with some foresight gain interest and gather products and become dealers and experts. An entire economy is built—even livelihoods are maintained from what was junk and is now treasure!

When you are first introduced to some pre-collectibles, you may feel some disbelief. A usual response is, "You've got to be kidding!" Other responses we've all heard are, "Who would have thought that people would want these nowadays?"and "My mom and dad (grandparents) had tons of these I used to just play with or take apart." Then you start searching the basement or garage of your folks' house. You may discover some items. You might even find the best of the best as far as what everybody is wanting in the new field. Then you find others, make contacts, and start picking for them and trading, maybe collect a few for yourself. Sometimes you get hooked. There is a fine line between picker-dealer and collector. Nostalgia is a big element at play here. People get emotionally attached to items and memories. Some of this stuff really gets important to them.

We find things that we had no idea existed. Things that were common at the time but now forgotten and disposed of. To piece together history is a very rewarding and exciting adventure for some.

As more and more get involved in the collecting of the items, some things gain higher popularity. Models become more valuable because they have a certain classic look. Features are pointed out in magazine articles. Rarity is discovered. The harder it is to find them, the more people want them, and values soar.

As I write this, some of the mentioned pre-collectibles are well on their way to becoming full-fledged collectibles. Some have prices bordering antiques. Look at pocket calculators or even slide rules. They both apparently started their rise to collecting within the scientific community. Values are rising, and good models are becoming scarce compared with a very short time ago.

The people who used these products daily in their work are familiar with the brands and the features and remember shopping for them. They also remember how much they wished they could have had certain ones but couldn't afford them at the time.

Now they find them at swap meets for pennies on the dollar. They have (by now) finished college and have careers. They also know the things that have replaced these old dinosaurs, but they still have a tender memory of the items and buy them because they still like them. They also recognize that today's manufacturing processes aren't as interesting as the old way. It's fun to look back at how they used to make stuff—bigger, heavy, ugly, beautiful, funny, and absolutely classic. They don't make stuff like that any more. You can go back in time when you assemble a small collection. You can see the innovation change model to model. The quality and craftsmanship and weight is different. The way it looked is different. It's historic, archaic, and wonderfully nostalgic.

Notice how competition drove innovation to more complex, more sleek, more massed produced items that are not, well, as interesting and good as the old stuff.

So, what will be the next craze, the next pre-collectible? How are you going to find it? Or how can you be involved and become an expert in the field once it is identified?

1. Be interested in it yourself. It has to hit a nerve.
2. Read magazines on collectibles.
3. Talk to people in clubs, other pickers, dealers etc. "What else do you collect?" or "What else is hot?"
4. Go to shows! Learn.
5. Send for mail order catalogs and lists from classified ads.
6. Read the wanted columns, take notes, and review them.
7. You might have knowledge and interest in an area that could initiate and drive a new market.
8. You may have a friend or relative who is crazy enough to have a large collection of just the stuff you are looking for.
9. Something neat you have already been buying every time you see it. I guarantee, someone somewhere else is too!

I had a conversation once with an old-timer. He said he had a radio repair shop that repaired large quantities of radios in the 1930s and 1940s. His company would take in jobs, fix them up and call later to find out the customer had replaced the radio with a newer and better or more modern and stylish radio. At this point, they were not interested in returning to pick up the repair. This might have been a cathedral radio or a bakelite or a floor console.

It was junk as far as this customer was concerned. It was also junk as far as this repairman was now concerned. He lost the profit of the repair bill. He couldn't possibly sell the old-fashioned used ones. He did not know that forty or fifty years later these things would be so precious. Besides, it would be impossible to warehouse them. Many trips were made to the landfill with large loads of wooden and plastic radios! Radios that are now considered classic. The repair bills were probably $10-12 a piece. Now these jewels are worth $100 to $500 or much more.

So we see now why they are collectible. The cycle that made them worthless, and subsequently tossed away, actually caused them to increase in value. The reason? They are now harder to find!

The growth of new collectors also helps the value climb. More and more are wanted and less and less are found. Supply and demand exactly. Tragic on the one hand, an antique or collectible is now a prize because a hundred or a thousand just like it have been disposed of, buried deeply in the trash heap.

# Chapter 9:
# Unique Opportunities

# Liquidators

Here's an interesting slant on picking, but it really works for some.

Many stores, distributors, and some manufacturers all accumulate extra unsold inventory. Inventory just sitting hurts the bottom line and ties up cash. Many times markets change and their customer's desires result in this unwanted merchandise. These companies get stuck with all sorts of excess product. It might be finished goods or the parts and pieces that they make the product with. Understand that these companies have written off or marked down these items to zero cost. You can usually offer any price and they will take it!

A liquidator can be one of the solutions for these companies. A liquidator comes in and offers some price way below the original price and takes the product and sells it somewhere in the market. Usually organized liquidator companies specialize in certain markets and seek out particular items regularly in those markets.

As a picker, you can approach this in several ways. If you have the cash and the customer base, you might want to approach a certain company and ask for a list of their dead or slow-moving inventory. Many times it is a quick computer report that will list what they paid for it originally. You can then contact other similar companies that might have current use for it and make a healthy profit.

Another way to work it is to contact one of the many organized liquidation companies informing them of your expertise in your field and ask about working on commission if you find certain products or buyers for their products. Some people even setup small companies with the word liquidator in their name, and send out cards and letters in quantity to stores and distributors telling them what they are looking for, and asking for samples. Then they contact the real liquidator with their find and put together a deal using other people's money and making a good profit!

Or you could simply be a liquidator, if you have the cash, the time, and the warehouse space to store and process the items you'll start finding.

# Stupid Crazy People!

As I am out picking, I see many other people picking some really weird stuff! I also see them pass by stuff I am looking anxiously for which amazes me! I've seen them carry around boxes and baskets of stuff I would not think twice about, and they are ecstatic and walk around as happy as larks! I'm sure people have seen me in the same way, feeling disbelief as they see my load of trash thinking I'm a crazy man.

All that glitters...

Am I stupid? Are they? If I can sell my find and double my money or triple I never feel crazy. If they're doing the same... wow!

It comes down to what and who you know about. It's based on your taste, experience and knowledge. It's who you know and the buyers you know that like what you find. It's the places you know where to sell the stuff. You may really like the products and have a good eye for it. You of course know its value, its rarity and can spot a classic. You have studied the books, know the history, and prices. I might have a hundred dollar book in my hand and another picker has a four hundred dollar doll or an expensive piece of glass. I know nothing about her find; she could care less about mine. We might even shake our heads when we see what turns the other person on. Interesting stuff, isn't it?

## All That Glitters May Still Be Gold

I know several people who deal in various stages of electronics collectibles who also make an absolute fortune in scrap metals and precious metals. Sure, they sell the old radios tubes and parts, but they have discovered there is gold and silver, platinum and palladium, copper and aluminum, and other scrap that is worth cash. Old p.c. boards and relays and parts have various amounts of valuable gold and silver contacts and plating. Various refiners will buy it in bulk and process it for a percentage if you assemble a large amount to ship to them. Often government auctions have bags and boxes and pallets of items containing such products

If you had about 200 lbs (about three small buckets of good clean pins), it would yield about seven ounces of gold. This is about $14 a pound before refining! Electronic relays have tiny contacts in them that have platinum, gold over silver, solid gold, and palladium metals.

If you are finding similar types of products, it would be well to research this area to find more profit in stuff you might have available.

## Buried Treasure—More Gold!

Yep, thars gold in them thar piles!

I was told by a friend of mine a great story of how he found gold out picking. He was at an estate sale that seemed like all the rest (actually, no estate sale is like any of the rest. That's what makes this so exciting!). As he was pawing through the items, he found an old box with some dental picks and tools and items. He thought they looked old and useful, so he bought the box. If I remember, it was like fifteen or twenty bucks. Guess what? As he was looking through the box (dare I say, "picker, picking through the dental picks") he found gold teeth—several of them. Somebody's grandpa was a dentist. He must have forgotten they were there. Well, they finally surfaced, were refined, and sold for hundreds of dollars. This really happened!

Well, then it happened to me about two months after my friend told me the story! I heard from a friend that someone he knew had some parts and old things I go after that he was wanting to get rid of. I made an appointment, saw the stuff, filled up my entire trunk for twenty five dollars and drove home. When I got there, I started going through the boxes, throwing away stuff, finding regular stuff, and an occasional neat thing or two. Then there it was—a gold dental bridge of about four teeth just shining up at me! It was in a box of old dirty hardware. This was about a half an ounce of gold!

It's out there! I guess it could be anywhere. If this much was found here in our little area, can you imagine all the garages and basements there are that have old junk in them that have little treasures like this, forgotten? I'll bet that in any large city there are hundreds of old coffee cans with some gold teeth or coins just sitting in them. Are you excited?

## Help Wanted: Dish Watcher

Did you know that there are companies that supply people with replacements for all of the priceless and irreplaceable dishes and glasses and silverware that is lost or broken?

One very large such supplier is Replacements Ltd. in Greensboro, NC. They have an immense warehouse filled with product where they process nearly 50,000 items per day. These can be recent or very old, antique or rare patterns. Their annual volume approaches $60,000,000 per year!

Where do they get many of the pieces to complete Grandma's set of china or silverware? From pickers! (Approximately 1500 of them, located all over the country!)

Replacements Ltd. has a very organized system and network of pickers that search for these items. The way they hire these pickers, is to sell them a subscription to a catalog and price guide they publish. This catalog lists thousands of patterns they are seeking and the prices they will pay if you find them.

This is just one of many such businesses (albeit, one of the largest) that provide a service like this and require an army of pickers to gather their inventory.

## How to Make Your Stuff Famous!

I know of a few collector/dealers who keep selling and selling the same item over and over and never really let it go. You see, these folks rent the antiques and collectibles in their collection for movie props!

I read an article about a collector who has a collection of over 50,000 modern artifacts. He rents items to photographers for props and makes about $50,000 a year doing so.

They simply make available to certain movie production companies in their area information on the stuff they specialize in and have in their collection. They usually have enough contacts and friends who collect that they become a valuable resource to the film industry.

These things, of course, are all done under the protection of a good contract. The renter is responsible for damage and loss.

They also offer historical research and consulting, so the film people get it right.

These folks have big budgets for this stuff and you can make quite a good fee for the rental of especially rare items. If they do buy the stuff from you, they usually pay exorbitant prices! Just think, you might be selling autographed photos of your collection to your friends!

## Gift Horses

When dealing with bulk collectibles know where to get there first. These types of deals are usually limited to friends or contacts calling out of the blue, "Hey, would you be interested in a bunch of ...?" If you have the time and are creative, you can search for some of these opportunities. Don't limit yourself to garage sales, swap meets, or even estate sales. Branch out looking for new and normally hidden sources. You might be interested in buying and selling electronic surplus. Call around, ask questions. Some places you might call are:

- Electronic manufacturing firms, or assembly houses
- Electronic distributors
- Scrap dealers
- College and universities surplus centers
- Government surplus depots and stores

• Local scrap refiners

Now if you contact these people, ask lots of questions and see where it leads you. You might get transferred many times. You might find dead ends. But, you will learn a great deal of information. You will start to pick up new terms you can use in the next conversation. You will soon seem like you know what you are talking about! You will get new names and contacts for your index.

By not giving up, you'll soon find the right person. This person could literally lead you to a gold mine—both in information and in products. Please note, this works both ways, whether you are buying or selling items. It also works for many industries and fields of interest, so get your yellow pages out, think of every likely resource you may have, and start calling. You never know where it might lead you!

## Specializing

Is there a hobby or interest you had when young you would like to resume?

Are you trained in a certain area that could lend an expertise to something collectible? (i.e., You are a computer technician and might go after the early computer or calculator market.)

Do you have special memories for certain old things of your past?

Do you have a large resource available, that is unique to your culture, or locality or historic area (i.e., Amish, pioneer, railroad, treasure, nearby historical manufacturer, etc.)?

Being a specialist in a particular field is the best and first way to enter the market. It is best to know all you can about one particular type of item. This could be glassware, toys, military memorabilia, or some really unique and off-the-wall subject.

Buy all of the books you can find and read about the subject. Subscribe to magazines dealing with the items. Join clubs, visit museums and other collectors and dealers. Ask questions and learn. Get familiar with prices, condition, etc. Recognize quality, model numbers, varieties, dates, and all you can about the best items. Absolutely know the rare and expensive pieces. Look for fakes, reissues, and reproductions. Become an expert and love it.

After this, you can become familiar with the spin off or closely-related fields of your specialty. The reason is, many of the collectors who go after the first level also collect and trade between other levels or that is, related products.

# Specializing

An example could be that your specialty is Victrolas and antique phonographs. A related or second level might be records or radios. Several collectors collect all of these. Next level may be televisions or telegraph items. Do you see how these are all related? Collectors then collect books for these fields.

Next, you should familiarize yourself with other general collectibles and antiques and with cash-producing finds. It is great when you're out looking for your particular items, and find a very salable cash-producing treasure. The beauty of it is that because it's not your thing, it isn't hard to let go. You can easily sell it and get money to invest in your specialty.

It is very handy to know a little about lots and lots of various industries. Commonly, book pickers work this way. After all, right next to the book that you want is likely a book you can sell quickly. Goodness, there is lots of stuff out there. I get excited writing about it!

So target and immerse yourself in your narrow field of interest. Then branch out. Open yourself up to other possibilities to make a profit, by searching the ads, looking for what all sorts of things people find interest in. You will find dealers and collectors that are anxious to get stuff you might have been passing up every day.

## Exporting

An interesting phenomenon is how the Japanese and other Asians are buying large amounts of vintage products from the USA. Items such as clothing, audio equipment, and collectibles of many types are being exported to eager collectors.

There is a fear by many US collectors that these products will all be sold and nothing will be left here to enjoy. In some cases it's true. Many items are just about off the US market completely.

The exporters argue that the US collector doesn't appreciate the items as much, apparent by their lack of willingness to pay the amount the Asians are. There is also a fear by some dealers that we better sell all we can right now because their overseas market will become saturated eventually and the prices will fall.

As I initially learned of the fervor that this market has, I wondered what the big secret was. My curiosity led me to talking to certain dealers and a few traveling Japanese buyers who come here to find products. The simple explanation is that it is a fad—almost a cult wish to have this stuff. Some pickers are making an extreme fortune in selling to these folks.

After World War II, the Japanese people were very poor (a typical wage per day was something like $1 per day for laborers). Lots of items made in Japan were shipped abroad to the USA and other wealthier countries. These people could not afford the items they both saw and those they would hear about. There is a very strong nostalgia for many of these items that they could not have (but wanted) in these earlier poorer times. They want those classics and that vintage stuff that they remember so fondly. The Japanese people have a different economy right now. They have a lot of disposable income and they spend it. The dollar and the yen are more even. They can afford it, and they pay a whole lot more for it! Those collectors who love this old US stuff have driven the prices up here and abroad—and most of it is just because they want to show off to their friends. If you look back a few short years ago, there was a lot of interest in the US for Soviet manufactured items. Here were products that the free world had never seen! This might give you a small example of the craze and fervor that the Asians have for US products, and why the demand might be so great.

I met a Japanese buyer who travels the US about three to four times a year. He has a truck he drives and a US warehouse. He knows the likely places to visit, places like we describe in this publication. He is essentially an international picker! This man is very organized, and he has a large clientele, and he has loads of cash with him. He's here for at least a month each trip, gathering and shipping stuff to his warehouse (at a friend's place). He then boxes it all up in a container and ships it home where his large warehouse and customers stand waiting.

Another exporter I know, who has a regular profession (actually a physician), has many of these international pickers from the orient visit him during the year. He knows what they want and gathers items from other pickers (I've sold him a few goodies) and warehouses them until they come shopping. He might have certain items he ships directly to his friends overseas. He tells me that the buyers have always got lots of cash and don't argue with him much on the price. I am sure that some negotiating takes place if there are large amounts purchased. Even at the seemingly high price that some of this stuff is sold for, the mark up gets quite large before the end Japanese consumer purchases it.

He gave me an example of a $1500 item. That is an item he can sell for $1500. This amount is the current market value that the item has in the USA. (You need to realize that the market value in the USA is inflated higher than in the recent past, because of the demand in the orient.) He might have bought it for $500 (if he's lucky) locally. The person who buys it from him will sell it for 30% to 50% higher or about double. He says it then goes into a store in Japan that cleans it up and resells it to an end consumer for much higher prices!

In Japan there is even a magazine devoted to Americana for fervent Japanese collectors. Another interesting side note is that there are many Japanese made items that were exported to the US that the Japanese collectors are desperately seeking. Where does it all end?

# Glossary

This is not just a regular old glossary. These are great idea pegwords. Review these terms occasionally and you'll find you get lots of good ideas and plans.

**Antiqued:** Not really antique, but new products that are made crudely, or rustic in mass production. Made to look like they are old and important. Usually decor items. Some antique stores have their entire store filled with this stuff.

**Bird-dogging:** A good bird-dogger can find a prize in the rough. You ask questions, get leads, dig a little bit further, try more ideas, and look in more places. This separates the great pickers from all of the regular folks. There is an old saying that says: "Even a blind hog finds an acorn once in awhile, but you've got to be rooting around!" You seem to have a nose for it. A good bird-dogger can also be called a good noser.

**Classic:** You can tell a classic when you see it. Classic items, to those who have developed a eye for them, seem to speak. It has to do with a combination of nostalgia, esthetics, a good knowledge of art and history, and refined tastes. Sometimes you get an appreciation from a description in a speech you hear or an article you read. You might have that appreciation grow by seeing an item that you had or saw as a child. Many times you can tell by heft, or weight combined with quality, details and craftsmanship. This along with period or age brings out the classic items.

**Closet Collector:** A closet collector is a very low profile collector. He or she collects for their own enjoyment, with not a lot of others knowing they collect much of anything. They are not too involved in clubs, shows, or other public displays with their collection. It might be a security concern they have or it could be they just prefer privacy. Once in awhile the only time the collection is seen is when the person's estate is for sale.

**Collectible:** Just about anything is, has been, or will be collectible. This can be items that are manufactured or found naturally. Certain people like to collect items within a specialty or several specialties.

**Dumpster Diving:** This is not really picking per se. But, I'm sure many items that end up for sale at swap meets and even some dealers shops may have been discovered in a dumpster somewhere. (Wash your hands often.)

**Early Birds:** These are folks who get the worms. You'll see ads for estate and yard sales that demand no early birds. Usually they mean the sale begins at 9:00 AM and they don't want people coming by at 7:00 AM before the crowd pounding on the door wanting to sneak in before everyone else. You should always plan your day to be out early in order to find the best stuff. It's always better to be polite at the sales.

**Esoteric:** This is the explanation given to people that means you are not in the loop or just would not understand pertaining to some collectors' interests. (I could give an example here, but I am afraid I'd upset someone).

**Faux:** Be familiar with this word. It means phony or fake. Some suppliers try to be sneaky and use this fancy word to hide the fact that their product is a rip-off or a reproduction.

**Feeding Frenzy:** This is when all of the pickers and others pile into a small area and push and shove and grab all the goodies before the other person can. Blood is pumping, eyes are looking back and forth, and grubby little fingers are frantically pawing through the goodies. It can be either exciting or exasperating.

**Flea Merchant:** If your livelihood is to buy items to sell at flea markets, here is your professional title. A flea merchant also finds gray market products, usually including factory seconds and overstock merchandise to sell. He might use these and other inventory to sell in other ways, such as small shops, out of his vehicle, etc. Some sell such items mail order, etc. You might be surprised to see how many manufacturers and distributors in your areas sell to flea merchants to dispose of their unwanted inventory.

**Forced Collectible:** This is a collectible that some smart or lucky marketer created. It is an illusion. Examples include those extremely hard-to-get items that become very scarce each Christmas-time. The supply somehow dried up and the media blows it out of proportion and the price and demand skyrockets! Examples include some famous dolls and little stuffed toys. Then the subsequent issues and models all benefit in the craze with inflated prices.

**High Grading:** To high-grade means you get in and get all of the very best stuff before anyone else gets a chance at it. This happens at estate sales by the family and others before the public sees it.

**Junkie:** A junkie has to buy something every day or he goes crazy. He needs to feed his passion. He will usually start shaking somewhat as he buys something fantastic. This can be a collector or a picker.

**Junkin:** This describes the activity of traveling around to various sites and sales and other likely spots looking for treasures in junk and trash and secondhand stuff. (See also yard sailing.)

**Junque or Junk:** I suppose junque is a deluxe or fancy style junk. I also suppose that junque has been rescued and displayed, where junk is sort of found as is and might not even be disposed of yet. Junk can still be good working items. Don't confuse it with garbage which can be wet and stinky and worthless. Trash, on the other hand, is anything that's been thrown away.

**Keystone:** This is a term that started in the jewelry trade. It means one half of retail or list price. This is what dealers consider a minimum profit margin or 100% markup. If you wholesale to dealers, be aware that they will need to at least double their cost before they put it out on the floor. Don't have a heart attack when you return to the store and see this higher price. (After all, you probably sold it to them and got five or ten times your cost!).

**Liquidator:** Someone who is in the business of buying and selling slow-moving merchandise. Some entrepreneurs find several interested buyers who will take everything they can turn up. They then contact likely distributors, dealers, and stores finding distressed merchandise at extremely marked down costs. Very profitable to a few creative people.

**Low balling or a low ball bid:** When you find certain stores or dealers or shows that have silent bids, you might try low balling occasionally. This means you go quite a bit lower than the value of the item, and probably much lower than you would normally bid yourself. You could also do this type of bidding on many more selections, which increases your chance of winning bids. When you do in fact win, you not only get more items, but they are at far better prices which increases your profits.

Low ball the bid even if you might not make a deal. Sometimes if you bid too high they will suspect an even higher value than it's worth. If you can bid and leave the deal open this is even better. This way you still have a chance to buy it, especially if you really want it.

**Mercenary:** Here are those who are only in it for the money. This is great if you make a living at picking, because you are constantly turning your inventory. Collectors can't understand how the mercenary can give up so many classic pieces. Mercenaries can't understand keeping the stuff if there is a buck to be made. Thank goodness it takes all types.

**Paper:** Paper is the documentation, catalogs, letters, books, booklets, advertisements, dealer information, manuals, literature, service information, labels, magazines, journals, diaries, photographs, posters, cards, specifications, price guides, histories, descriptions, copies, autographs, manuscripts, reprints, correspondence, and other paper items about or found with old products. This stuff is also very collectible and valuable. It is also wonderful reference material as you study and research your special topics and fields of interest.

**Parlaying:** This is when you start with a dollar and buy something worth more, then sell it up and up with more items doubling your original investment. You also get the benefit of learning more about collectibles and antiques as you handle more pieces and can relate with more prices.

You know what? You can parlay a dollar, doubling it just twenty times and end up with a million dollars. If you start out with a thousand it only takes ten steps! In one day, you can easily parlay your money and finds a couple of times. It's a bunch of fun to do. It doesn't work if you make bad purchase decisions or don't know how to sell, or if you want to keep everything you buy.

**Picker:** A professional merchant, scrounger, collector, finder, or forager specializing in one or more fields. An expert in the values and market of old, useful, and valuable items. One who is constantly looking for antiques and other collectibles or even industrial products. Some of these items can be extremely valuable or historically important, in what many people consider junk. The picker finds items for himself or to resell for a profit to dealers and to collectors. A true harvester of good items of value.

**Pre-Chasing:** If you have an opportunity to preview items included in auctions to be held, and then go find a customer for those items before they are even your property, you are pre-chasing. When you bid on the items, you already know for sure how much your customer will pay and how many they will buy from you. An awful lot of smart profit is made every day this way. There are folks who make a very comfortable living doing just this. Some crafty businessmen never even touch the product. They bid, buy, and then they ship it off to their customer and keep the profit.

You need to realize, however, that there could be many other bidders in attendance at the auction that are doing the same thing. They might have even contacted the same potential customer you did!

**Pre-Estate Sale:** This is a sell-off of an estate or collection before the public has a chance to even know about it. You might just luck upon it or by word of mouth hear about it. Sometimes you are contacted because of advertising you do or because of your reputation in a certain market. You might get a call like; "You need to call Mrs. Doe. She said her basement is full of her husband's collection which she wants to get rid of." If it would have gone on an estate sale, you'd probably never have a chance. If you are fortunate, you might go view the collection, make a deal, pay for and pack away the entire lot. You might have the opportunity to select and purchase just the best pieces (see high-grading). You usually have a wonderful time sorting through all of the stuff at your own pace because there is no competition fighting you for the best stuff. In fact, your competition will probably never hear about it unless you tell them.

**Pre-selecting:** This is when you are given a chance to purchase items before an auction is held or before a public advertised sale. This happens rarely, usually for family or friends or employees. Often special customers who have a good buying record are invited to do preselecting. When items are auctioned from government agencies, they often allow preselecting to adjoining agencies. Hate it if you're not invited, go for it if you are!

**Rescue:** The act of finding vintage and classic collectors' items before they find a way to the landfill.

**Salted Auction:** A salted auction is where the auction firm will bring in a load of items from many different sources, even many commercially available products. For example, if you go to an "estate sale" and find twenty oriental rugs or a gun collection being sold by a third party. The extra items are out of place but convenient for the auction company to sell a bit extra.

**Salvager or Scrapper:** A recycler. Many times, when processing junk and products, some refuse has some scrap or salvage value. Metals and even precious metals can be obtained and bring extra profits. Sometimes, just piling it up and occasionally turning it in for cash can be worthwhile. Salvaging not only pertains to metals but can include any material that has residual value that can be recycled.

**Scalper:** A scalper knows his product and what his customer wants and needs. He asks and gets top dollar. He is a mercenary.

**Scouts:** Used booksellers have been naming their pickers scouts. Book scouts are a very valuable resource for book dealers to fulfill their constant need for inventory. Many book scouts are university students trying to augment their income. The book market is divided into countless specialties which require study and experience. Knowledgeable book scouts can do extremely well. Scouts work the same places as antique and collectible pickers—estate sales, thrift stores, etc.

**Scrounger, Scavenger, Rummager:** These terms tend to describe picking at the lower end of the scale. These could be aimless pack rats who buy stuff just because. But, realize this: they are still your competition. They will buy items before you get a chance and might get in your way.

**Smalls:** Many times you will see in antique stores a glass case with tiny antiques and collectibles. These are sometimes overlooked items that sometimes have a very good value and profit margin. Look for these smalls when you are out and about. It might be a little toy or an advertising specialty or just an old knickknack.

**Vintage:** This has to do with the age of the item. Vintage, relating to fine aged wine, has given an interesting accent to all kinds of collectibles. So now, vintage clothing, vintage toys, vintage cars, etc. now mean more that just old stuff. It's something made long ago. It was from a certain period. It is collectible and valuable.

**Yard Sailing:** Usually lots of fun, but often not too productive. When you get up early and go out randomly hitting yard sales and garage sales, and maybe even luck upon an estate sale, you are yard sailing. This is all chance and luck. You could be surprised and find a real treasure, or waste lots of time and gas.

An improved method is to "chart a course", based on what interesting ads you see in the classifieds. If you also focus on areas of the city that typically are old and established, you'll do better. The course always beats luck and chance. You can still stop randomly at certain sales you see along the way. You have to get out early, as it's all over by noon. (I think if someone could get it started, they might have success with ads that say "late afternoon yard sale, come here after you're through with the early sales.")

# Appendix A: Patent Dates

Here is a list of patent numbers along with a date of issue. This list might be helpful to you as you look for old products that have patent numbers marked on them.

| Year | Number | Year | Number | Year | Number |
|------|--------|------|--------|------|--------|
| 1870 | 98,460 | 1901 | 664,827 | 1932 | 1,839,190 |
| 1871 | 110,617 | 1902 | 690,385 | 1933 | 1,892,633 |
| 1872 | 122,304 | 1903 | 717,521 | 1934 | 1,944,449 |
| 1873 | 134,504 | 1904 | 748,567 | 1935 | 1,985,878 |
| 1874 | 146,120 | 1905 | 778,834 | 1936 | 2,026,510 |
| 1875 | 158,350 | 1906 | 808,618 | 1937 | 2,066,309 |
| 1876 | 171,641 | 1907 | 839,799 | 1938 | 2,101,004 |
| 1877 | 185,813 | 1908 | ? | 1939 | 2,142,080 |
| 1878 | 198,733 | 1909 | 908,436 | 1940 | 2,185,170 |
| 1879 | 211,078 | 1910 | 945,010 | 1941 | 2,227,418 |
| 1880 | 223,211 | 1911 | 980,178 | 1942 | 2,268,540 |
| 1881 | 236,137 | 1912 | 1,013,095 | 1943 | 2,307,007 |
| 1882 | 251,685 | 1913 | 1,049,326 | 1944 | 2,338,081 |
| 1883 | 269,820 | 1914 | 1,083,267 | 1945 | 2,366,154 |
| 1884 | 291,016 | 1915 | 1,123,212 | 1946 | 2,391,856 |
| 1885 | 310,163 | 1916 | 1,166,419 | 1947 | 2,413,675 |
| 1886 | 333,494 | 1917 | 1,210,389 | 1948 | 2,433,824 |
| 1887 | 355,291 | 1918 | 1,251,458 | 1949 | 2,457,797 |
| 1888 | 375,720 | 1919 | 1,290,027 | 1950 | 2,492,944 |
| 1889 | 395,305 | 1920 | 1,326,899 | 1951 | 2,536,016 |
| 1890 | 418,665 | 1921 | 1,364,063 | 1952 | 2,580,379 |
| 1891 | 443,987 | 1922 | 1,401,948 | 1953 | 2,624,016 |
| 1892 | 466,315 | 1923 | 1,440,362 | 1954 | 2,664,562 |
| 1893 | 488,976 | 1924 | 1,478,996 | 1955 | 2,698,431 |
| 1894 | 511,744 | 1925 | 1,521,590 | 1956 | 2,728,913 |
| 1895 | 531,619 | 1926 | 1,568,040 | 1957 | 2,775,762 |
| 1896 | 552,502 | 1927 | 1,612,790 | 1958 | 2,813,567 |
| 1897 | 574,369 | 1928 | 1,654,521 | 1959 | 2,866,973 |
| 1898 | 596,467 | 1929 | 1,696,897 | 1960 | 2,919,443 |
| 1899 | 616,871 | 1930 | 1,742,181 | | |
| 1900 | 640,167 | 1931 | 1,787,424 | | |

# Appendix B: Condition of Items

You have heard the phrase, I'm sure, that for a business to be successful, the most important items are: Location, Location, Location!

For pickers, collectors, and dealers remember this: Condition, Condition, Condition! The better, most valuable items collectors want are those in the best physical shape. The closer to original, the better (and the more expensive).

Let's try and describe condition:

**10/Mint In Box/(MIB).** Just as if it were purchased yesterday. The item is exceptional. Without flaw. (If it is a device, such as a machine or a radio, it may not function because of the age of the internal components. It still is considered mint condition.) Has all of the original papers and packing. The value of an item in this condition will probably be much higher than listed in any book price guide, maybe even several times the listed price. Could be historically important.

**9/Mint.** As listed above but might be missing the box, or the box might be very worn or falling apart. Packing might be gone, etc. The actual unit is, however, mint. The value could still be above the price guides' listings.

**8/New in box/New Old Stock/(NIB, NOS).** These items might be new, never used, but may have been around a bit. They have lots of fingerprints, boxes are dilapidated, packaging has water stains and mildew. Still new, but obviously not mint. Might be the best possible to obtain, however.

**7/Excellent/ or Choice.** Very sought after item. Like new, but has been used. It's been handled, but carefully. Has dust, polish marks, fingerprints, but otherwise fine.

**6/Nice.** Has a little more use than our item above. It may have discoloration or minor flaws. It's still a fine piece to have displayed in any collection. No real wear, or any damage.

**5/Very Good.** This is a good piece that is salable and collectible. It may show use and wear but displays nicely.

**4/Average.** A good representation of the collectible. Still collectible and displayable. It may have one or more blemishes. Usually traded as a better piece comes along.

**3/Fair.** Trade stock only. May have a crack. May have been painted, or have rust, etc. May have been modified from the original.

**2/Worn.** Pretty bad shape. Someone may want it. Several cracks or bad cabinet, etc. May be repairable or restorable if someone wants a real project. Still all there.

**1/Parts unit.** Has major parts and pieces missing. Incomplete. Good to use if rebuilding something else, as it is beyond repair by itself.

Other conditions described say "as found" or "untested", which could mean anything.

Just for fun we might toss in a "scale of stuff"

1. Brand new—current items
2. New, discontinued items
3. New, surplus—government, military, etc.
4. New, old stock—vintage
5. Second hand—working
6. Second hand—broken, fixable
7. Used, worn—limited use left
8. Junque—interesting junk
9. Junk—metal, parts, pieces, limited value
10. Scrap—reclaim value
11. Trash—mixed with other wastes
12. Waste—literally wasted, may include some good, but unre-claimable
13. Garbage—wet, stinky, hazardous

# Appendix C: The Re's

Be familiar with the following descriptions. It could mean the difference between a very valuable or valueless piece.

Restored: Restored (if properly done) actually brings the item to like new or original condition. This is usually accomplished by using parts from another unit from the same time period which is entirely proper. All parts of the unit must be original. The proper restoration of certain products can be a very fulfilling and rewarding experience. Besides, it adds value to the item.

Repaired: This may be a replaced part, or gluing, or other craftsmanship that has been done to help the item. Note that a replaced part may be new and not as original. If you intend on keeping or collecting a very old item, it is better to repair it as soon as you can, rather than waiting. The reason to repair it now is, it may not be possible to do so in the future. Parts and pieces might not be available. In fact parts might be finding their way to the landfills in a higher rate than the finished products. People don't know what to do with them. So repair stuff you intend on keeping now, it will be better and less expensive to do it now. Note: Certain devices have been modified to work, or to work better than original. This may detract from or even destroy the value of the object.

Refinished: Usually pertaining to the paint or finish that may have been worn or damaged. Depending on the item and the quality of the job, this can ruin or restore an antique. Many collectors and dealers prefer to have the finish untouched. Well-meaning amateurs have botched many a fine antique, especially when they try to age it, by antiquing it with improper finishes, etc. It's like those stories we hear of the $100,000 piece being refinished. The new owner doesn't like the original finish and strips it off. Now it's only worth $10,000!

Proper cleaning and proper applications of waxes and polishes can improve the otherwise poor finish. Some popular polishes can be detrimental as they contain ingredients, like silicone, that will make it very difficult to refinish properly in the future.

Refurbished: A refurbished item could be one that is thrown together to make it look more valuable than it is. It may have some improper hardware or pieces attached to help it sell or something done just to make it presentable to the customer. An unwary customer might not find out what has been done until much later.

Reproduction: This could pertain to the entire item or to just various pieces of the item. It means fake or faux. Be careful when buying certain items, that might look too good to be true. It might be a reproduction. Some popular antiques have certain parts that wear or break often to require replacement parts be made to repair them. Small businesses thrive on making these reproduction items. If you are aware of certain parts being repros that is okay. It's when you try and pass it off as all original that it's bad.

Replaced: You might find a nice antique that has a part off a different antique that fits and looks presentable. Sometimes various manufacturers have pieces that fit from subsequent issues of the same product. It's sort of like car parts that fit the older style. If you're not careful, you'll end up with a sort of "Frankenstein" piece. It's all antique, just not correct. This can have an effect on the price and value of the piece.

Recycling: The last effort we should make is the recycling of the stuff we get. This might be as simple as keeping certain parts to be replacements all the way to the metal scrap value of what is left.

Finally, although not starting with Re is cleaning. Nothing can add dollars to your investment as quickly as a good cleaning. Many times dust and grime cover some beautiful features otherwise unappreciated. A good polish can remove some pretty ugly flaws. Vacuuming can remove dust, mouse droppings, and hair that often infest the innards of all kinds of antiques. Learn what types of cleaners and polishes work best on various types of materials.

**Serial Number Zero!** Another item to watch for would be those collectibles which are actual prototypes. Once in a great while, the original inventor that produced a product which now is deemed collectible, still has in his possession the prototype of the product. These can be very valuable because they are one-of-a-kind and may have some historical interest. This, along with the original documentation and drawings and letters, and inventor's handwritten notes, could be quite an important find.

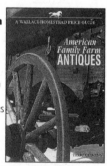